L. & F. FUNCKEN

ARMS and UNIFORMS

Other titles in this series

Arms and Uniforms I–Ancient Egypt to the 18th Century

Arms and Uniforms II–18th Century to the Present Day

The Napoleonic Wars I

Liliane and Fred Funcken

THE NAPOLEONIC WARS

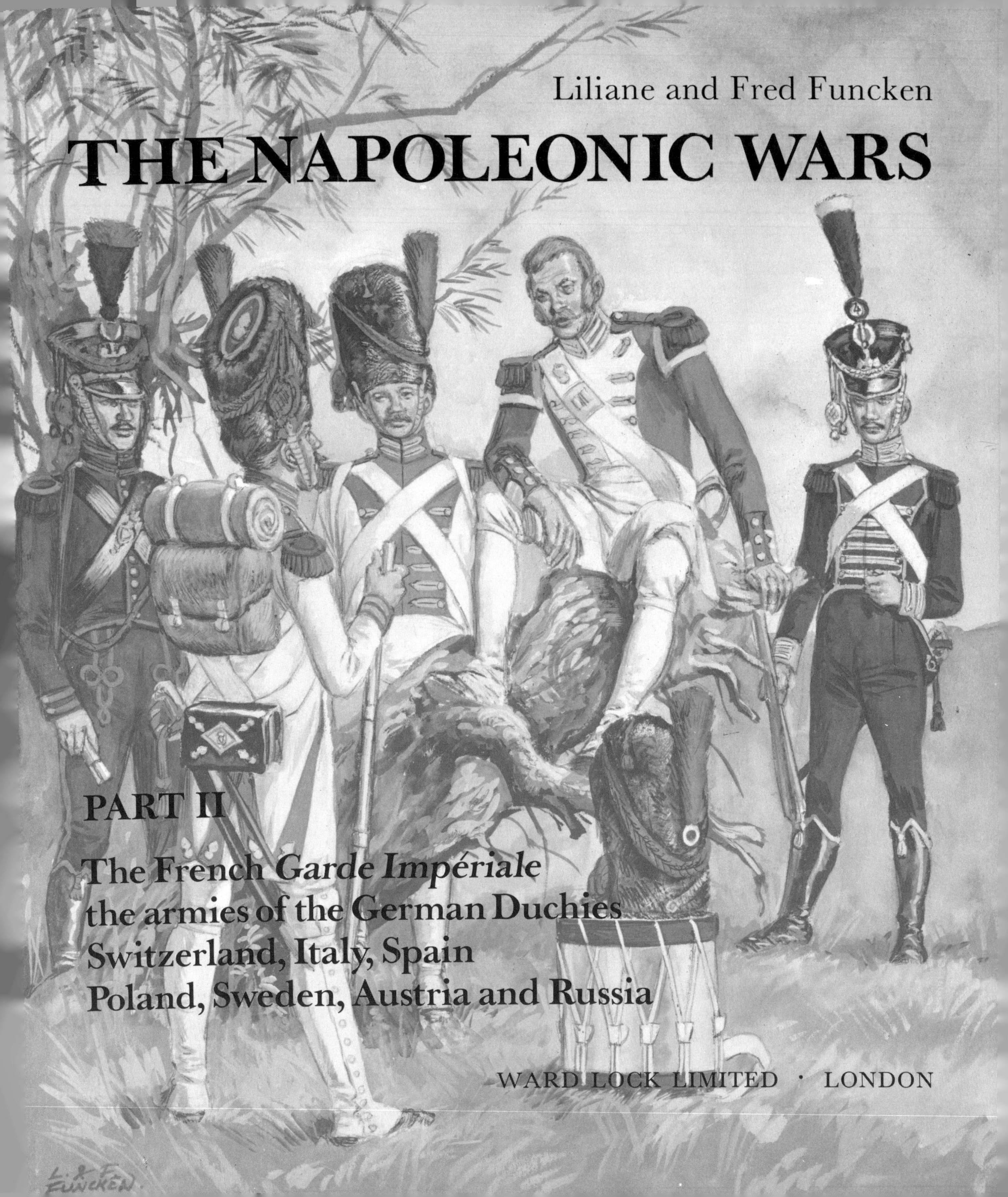

PART II

The French *Garde Impériale* the armies of the German Duchies Switzerland, Italy, Spain Poland, Sweden, Austria and Russia

WARD LOCK LIMITED · LONDON

ISBN 0 7063 1407 7

First published in Great Britain 1973 by Ward Lock Limited, 116 Baker Street, London, W1M 2BB

Designed by Conal Buck

Text filmset in 12/16pt Baskerville by V. Siviter Smith & Co Ltd

Printed and bound by Casterman, Tournai, Belgium

Contents

Introductory Note

In the section dealing with the French Army, we have, in general, retained the French titles for the various ranks. The organisation of the French Army was different from that of the British Army so that, although the actual words can be translated, their meaning is not necessarily the same. Thus in the British Army, except in the Foot Guards, a Major was the second-in-command of a battalion whereas in the French Army, the equivalent rank, *chef de bataillon,* commanded the battalion and the title 'major' was not applied to him. Similarly the *maréchal de camp,* later called a *général de brigade,* was not the same as a Brigadier-General or a Brigadier.

Likewise in most cases we have retained the actual names of the regiments and corps as to transpose them into English merely makes them look grotesque without conveying any greater meaning. Some, too, cannot be translated. A good example is what the Germans called a *Leib-Regiment,* which in straight translation becomes 'Body Regiment'. What the term actually means, however, is a Regiment of which the Colonel is the King. To twist this into 'The King's' or 'The King's Own' does not produce a satisfactory answer, for the significance, in English, is entirely different. We still have 'King's' Regiments in the British Army to-day, although our Monarch is a Queen.

THE GARDE IMPÉRIALE

Napoleon raised the *Garde Impériale* on 18 May 1804. This was not simply a change of name of the former *Garde Consulaire,* which was responsible for the security of the Central Government, but constituted a distinct and special corps of the Army designed for his personal protection. Only the most important parts of the *Garde Consulaire* were retained.

The Emperor never allowed anything to be published about this private army. Even the Gazette never printed a line on the subject, so that his enemies would never discover how it was that the Little Corporal bound these chosen men to himself.

The unending wars necessitated repeated increases in the establishment, particularly after the disaster of 1812. In 1804, the strength was 9,775, in 1809 theoretically 23,924, and in 1815, 126,850. However in January 1814, the actual strength was 17,498.

GRENADIERS À PIED I

1. Grenadier, service dress
2. Sergeant, full dress
3. Grenadier, full dress
4. Crown of bearskin after 1807
5. Crown before 1807
6. Detail of turnback
7. Grenadier's hat

Composition of the Garde Impériale:

GENERAL STAFF		PUPILLES
Corps of Grenadiers à Pied:		Cavalry:
Grenadiers à Pied:	Old Guard	Grenadiers à Cheval
Fusiliers Grenadiers:	Middle Guard	Chasseurs à Cheval
Tirailleurs Grenadiers:	Young Guard	Mamelukes
Conscrits Grenadiers:	Young Guard	Chevau-légers Lanciers
Flanqueurs Grenadiers:	Young Guard	Dragoons
Veterans	Old Guard	Éclaireurs
Corps of Chasseurs à Pied:		Gendarmes d'Élite
Chasseurs à Pied:	Old Guard	Gendarmes d'Ordonnance
Fusiliers Chasseurs:	Middle Guard	Artillery
Tirailleurs Chasseurs:	Young Guard	Engineers
Conscrits Chasseurs:	Young Guard	Transport
Flanqueurs Chasseurs:	Young Guard	Marines
National Guard:	Young Guard	Body Guards
Training Battalion at Fontainebleau		

1
2
3
4
5
6
7
L. & F. FUNCKEN

Whatever increases in strength were made to the *Garde Impériale,* the two Corps of Infantry, the Grenadiers and the Chasseurs, carried on all the time, each remaining at the same strength.

The Old Corps, namely the *Grenadiers à Pied,* the *Chasseurs à Pied,* the *Fusiliers Grenadiers,* the Foot Artillery, the Horse Artillery, the *Grenadiers à Cheval,* the *Chasseurs à Cheval,* the Artillery Train, the Supply Train and the *Gendarmes d'Élite,* wore their hair in a queue. All the other Corps cut their hair short.

The general modification of uniforms in 1812[1] did not apply to the *Garde Impériale,* apart from the Young Guard, and then only as an afterthought.

The Grenadiers à Pied

By an order dated 29 July 1804, the Grenadiers of the Consular Guard were reorganised into a Headquarters, two battalions of Grenadiers and one battalion of *Vélites*. These last were young soldiers, earmarked for service with the Grenadiers or the Chasseurs after completing their training. They served alongside their seniors and wore the same uniform. A *Vélite* had to have an annual income of not less than 200 francs.

There were eight companies in a Grenadier battalion, but only five in a *Vélite* battalion. A Grenadier company was commanded by a Captain with one First Lieutenant, two Second Lieutenants, one Sergeant-Major, four Sergeants, one Quartermaster-Sergeant, eight Corporals, two Pioneer-Corporals, eighty Grenadiers and two Drummers. A *Vélite* company was commanded by a Lieutenant with one Second Lieutenant, one Sergeant-Major, four Sergeants, one Quartermaster-Sergeant, eight Corporals, 172 *Vélites* and two Drummers.

On 18 May 1811, a second regiment of *Grenadiers à Pied*

1. See Volume 1.

GRENADIERS À PIED II

1. Officer, full dress (summer, 1804)
2. Pioneer sergeant, full dress (1810)
3. Grenadier, marching order (1807)
4. Officer, service dress (1806)
5. Ensign, full dress (1811)
6. Grenadier, marching order (1815)
7. Corporal in greatcoat

GARDE
IMPERIALE
L'EMPEREUR
DES FRANCAIS
AU 1er REGIMENT
DES GRENADIERS
A PIED
1
2
3
4
5
6
7
L. & F. FUNCKEN

was raised, with a strength of 1,600 men. To be eligible for the *Grenadiers à Pied,* a man had to have served as a non-commissioned officer or private in the Infantry of the Line or the Light Infantry for five years, be not less than five feet, nine inches in height, be of good character as well as being an efficient soldier and to have served in at least two campaigns. There were other requirements, too. Service with the *Garde Impériale* was a much sought-after honour, but not all comers were accepted.

The Grenadiers, who had won for themselves a glorious name, were disbanded after the Battle of Waterloo. Some took service in the *Garde Royale,* others emigrated to Turkey, Greece and America. The majority, however, returned home, where they had to endure the slights and pin-pricks of the local jacks-in-office.

The Dutch Grenadiers

After the union of Holland and France in 1810, Napoleon incorporated his brother's (Louis Bonaparte, King of Holland) Regiment of Guards into the *Garde Impériale* as the 2nd Regiment of *Grenadiers à Pied.* They were generally known as the *Grenadiers Hollandais* or Dutch Grenadiers. When the second regiment of *Grenadiers à Pied* was raised in 1811, the Dutch Grenadiers were re-numbered as the 3rd Regiment. The 3rd Grenadiers retained their former white uniform, but removed the loops round the button-holes and on the collar, and adopted the buttons of the *Garde Impériale.* They wore the bearskin without a plate.

The hat that the Dutch Grenadiers wore in undress, following the fashion of their French comrades, was discontinued in marching order.

A certain Captain Coignet recounts in his memoirs that, in 1809, when the French forces crossed the Danube and occupied the Island of Lobau below Vienna, the Emperor ordered the Grenadiers to wear their bearskins. In the hurry of having to get their bearskins out of the bags in which they were carried on the top of their packs, they threw their hats

3rd GRENADIERS
('EX-HOLLANDAIS')

1. Sergeant-Major, walking-out dress (1811)
2. Officer, full dress (1812)
3. Grenadier, full dress (1812)
4. Crown of bearskin

1
2
3
4

into the river and thenceforth they always wore the bearskin with neither plume nor festoon, both on the march and in action. With their wicker-covered water-bottles slung over one shoulder, 'fully armed and equipped, with forty rounds, the grenadier carried about 65 pounds, for this included his full dress which was essential for his final success in the capitals that he visited in the guise of a conqueror'.[2]

The Dutch Grenadiers took part in the Russian Campaign, and were taken prisoner almost to a man in November 1812. The Regiment was disbanded in 1813, and those who escaped capture were transferred to the two French Grenadier Regiments.

The Fusiliers Grenadiers

An order, dated 19 September 1806 at Saint-Cloud, authorised the raising of a regiment which was known as the *Fusiliers Grenadiers,* which had a strength of 1,600 men and ranked immediately after the Old Guard. Together with the *Fusiliers Chasseurs*,[3] they formed what was later called the Middle Guard.

It was formed from the two battalions of *Vélites* Grenadiers. In order to bring it up to strength, that is to four battalions, each of four companies of 120 men; reinforcements were found from the Departmental Reserve Companies and by conscription.

The uniform of the *Fusiliers Grenadiers* was the same as that of the Grenadiers, except for a difference in the epaulette, also they wore a shako with white worsted side chevrons instead of the bearskin. Likewise, the officers dressed like the Grenadier officers, but with a shako ornamented with gold lace and cords.

The *Fusiliers Grenadiers* were organised in the same way as the regiments of the Old Guard, nor were they in any way inferior to them as soldiers.

2. *Les Derniers Jours de la Grande Armée* by Captain Hippolite de Mauduit.
3. See the section on *Chasseurs à Pied.*

FUSILIERS GRENADIERS

1. Marching order (1810)
2. Full dress (1806-14)
3. Other ranks' shako
4. Officer's shako; after 1813 a less elaborate model, without cords or tassels, was adopted
5. Epaulette
6. Eagle shako-plate

3
4
5
1
2
6
L. & F. FUNCKEN

Tirailleurs Grenadiers

At Valladolid on 16 January 1809, the Emperor ordered the formation of a number of new regiments that later became the Young Guard, they were made up of conscripts who had to be both fit and literate. A second regiment was raised on 25 April 1809, the third and fourth regiments on 10 February 1811 and the fifth and sixth in August. By 1813, there were thirteen of these regiments and, in 1814, nineteen. In 1815, only six regiments remained.

Conscrits Grenadiers

Further units of the Young Guard, the two regiments of *Conscrits Grenadiers,* were raised on 29 and 31 March 1809; these men also had to be fit and literate. They were put on the same footing as the regiments of the line. In 1810, these two regiments were converted into *Tirailleurs Grenadiers,* ranking after the two existing units.

Flanqueurs Grenadiers

The regiment of *Flanqueurs de la Garde* was formed on 4 September 1811, and was recruited from the sons of employees of the *Eaux et Forêts*.[4] They wore green coatees, the colour commemorating the forests of their birth, the lapels were square. The regiment was disbanded in 1814 and the men were dispersed among the regiments of the line.

Tirailleurs

The 1st and 2nd Regiments of *Tirailleurs Grenadiers* and the 1st and 2nd Regiments of *Conscrits Grenadiers* were converted, on 30 December 1810, into the 1st, 2nd, 3rd and 4th Regiments of *Tirailleurs;* a fifth and sixth regiments were added on 18 May 1811. In 1813, there were thirty-one regiments. Although newly-formed, these regiments were incorporated into the Young Guard. They wore the uniform of the *Tirailleurs Grenadiers,* but with the festoon of the shako

4. The governmental Department responsible for the Waterways and Forests.

TIRAILLEURS GRENADIERS

1. Subaltern
2. Private, 1st Regiment, full dress
3. Cartridge-pouch
4. N.C.O.'s turnback
5. N.C.O.'s epaulette
6. Rank and Files' turnback
7. Shako (1811)

8–13. Shakos showing the pompoms worn by each regiment (1st–6th). After April 1813, they all wore red pompoms

1
2
3
4
5
6
7
8
9
10
11
12
13
L. & F. FUNCKEN

coloured red instead of white. They strove to uphold the traditions of the Young Guard.

Veterans

The Veteran Company was raised on 8 March 1802 and was incorporated into the *Garde Impériale* on 29 July 1804. It was composed of soldiers of the *Garde* who had become unfit for service on account of wounds or sickness. Originally, the number was set at one hundred, but this was later doubled. To be eligible for membership, a soldier had to have served in the *Garde Impériale* for at least three years. The Company was quartered in the Château of Versailles.

The Chasseurs à Pied

Apart from minor differences, the *Chasseurs à Pied* evolved in much the same way as the *Grenadiers à Pied*, whose development we have just studied.

Originally, the minimum height was put at five feet and nine inches, but it was lowered to five feet and six inches later. Previous service of five years in the Light Infantry and experience in two campaigns were further conditions required of volunteers for the *Chasseurs*. The order establishing the *Garde Impériale*, dated 29 July 1804, authorised the formation of the 1st Regiment and directed that it should have the same establishment as the Grenadiers, with a Headquarters, two battalions of *Chasseurs* and one of *Vélites*. A second regiment was raised with a similar establishment on 15 April 1806.

For a very short time, at the First Restoration in 1814,

CONSCRIPTS & CHASSEURS GRENADIERS

1. Conscript grenadier (1809)
2. Flanquer grenadier (1811)
3. Veteran
4. Shako of an Officer of the Conscrits and Chasseurs Grenadiers
5. Turnback, Conscrits Grenadiers
6. Turnback, Chasseurs Grenadiers

4
5
6
1
2
3
L. & F. FUNCKEN

they became the *Corps Royal des Chasseurs à Pied de France* (Royal Corps of French Chasseurs à Pied), but, when Napoleon returned from Elba in 1815, they were reorganised into four regiments. After Waterloo, they were withdrawn behind the Loire and were disbanded.

The uniform of the *Chasseurs à Pied* was very like that of the *Grenadiers,* the principal difference being that their bearskins had no plates and no coloured patch on top. A look at the illustrations will show the other differences.

Marching order included either the hat or the bearskin less its ornamentation and, according to the season, the coatee and loose white trousers or the greatcoat and loose blue trousers.

Fusiliers Chasseurs

The regiment of *Fusiliers Chasseurs* was raised on 15 December 1806, and consisted of two battalions of *Vélites* Chasseurs. Together with the regiment of *Fusiliers Grenadiers,* the *Fusiliers Chasseurs* formed what became known as the Middle Guard. To bring the regiment up to strength, namely, four battalions each of four companies of 120 men, reinforcements were found from the Departmental Reserve Companies and by conscription. In 1813, two companies were added to each battalion.

The uniform was the same as for the *Chasseurs à Pied,* except that the bearskin was replaced by a shako with a brass plate in the form of an Eagle, brass chin-scales and a white festoon. The officer's shako was of velvet, embroidered in gold. In marching order, the dress was the same as that of the Chasseurs, but with a green pompom.

Tirailleurs Chasseurs

The two regiments of *Tirailleurs Chasseurs* were formed at the same time and had the same establishment as the *Tirailleurs Grenadiers*; their uniform, authorised on 10 May 1809, differed only in having green eagles embroidered on

CHASSEURS À PIED

1. Marching order
2. Full dress
3. Officer's service dress coatee
4. Officer's hat
5. Turnback, other ranks

3
4
5
1
2

the turn-backs, green shoulder-straps piped with scarlet, and a green plume on the shako.

On 30 December 1810, the title was changed from *Tirailleurs Chasseurs* to *Voltigeurs*, and the collar became buff with blue piping. In 1813, both regiments replaced the plume on the shako by a green pompom.

Conscrits Chasseurs

The two regiments of *Conscrits Chasseurs* were formed at the same time as the *Conscrits Grenadiers*. The uniform was the same as that of the *Tirailleurs Chasseurs*, except that the turn-backs were blue with green hunting horns. The *Conscrits Chasseurs* were converted into *Voltigeurs* on 30 December 1810, and adopted their uniform. They were numbered as the 3rd and 4th Regiments.

Flanqueurs Chasseurs

The *Flanqueurs Chasseurs* were formed as a single regiment on 23 March 1813 and were incorporated into the Young Guard on 26 December following. There were six companies in each battalion. The *Flanqueurs* were disbanded in 1814, and the men were transferred to the Infantry of the line. The uniform was a green coatee of the same cut as that of the *Voltigeurs*. They did not carry the short sword.

Voltigeurs

On 30 December 1810, the 1st and 2nd Regiments of *Tirailleurs Chasseurs* were renamed *Voltigeurs*, and, at the same time, the 1st and 2nd Regiments of *Conscrits Chasseurs* became the 3rd and 4th *Voltigeurs*. No alteration was made in their establishments, but the uniform was changed.

A fifth regiment was raised on 18 May 1811, and a sixth on 26 August. Then, on 15 February 1813, the National Guard Regiment of the *Garde Impériale* became the 7th *Voltigeurs*. The 8th Regiment was raised on 25 March 1813, and the 9th to 13th Regiments on 3 April. Finally, on 21 January 1814, the 14th to 19th Regiments were raised.

FUSILIERS & TIRAILLEURS CHASSEURS

1. Fusilier Chasseur
2. Tirailleur Chasseurs
3. Light Infantry
4. Epaulette, Fusiliers Chasseurs
5. Turnback, Tirailleurs Chasseurs
6. Collar of alternative pattern, Voltigeurs
7. Alternative pattern, turnback, Voltigeurs and Tirailleurs

1
2
3
4
5
6
7
L. & F. FUNCKEN

The National Guard

These soldiers, whom we have already mentioned, were enlisted for service with the *Garde Impériale* and were formed into a regiment of four battalions. Together with the other National Guard Regiments, they had defended the coast of Flanders and the Channel coast in 1809. In this way, Napoleon rewarded the men from the North of France.

The Training Battalion at Fontainebleau

The Fontainebleau Training Battalion was designed to produce experienced non-commissioned officers for the regiments of the Young Guard but, after the terrible losses in 1812 and 1813 and since Saint-Cyr could not find enough replacements, Fontainebleau provided second lieutenants for the whole army.

The Pupilles

In Holland during the reign of Louis Bonaparte, two battalions of Royal *Vélites* had been raised from among abandoned children, the sons of officers and other ranks killed or died on service, and orphans. When Holland was united with France in 1811, Napoleon decided that the *Petits Hollandais*, as these battalions were known, should be transferred to the *Garde Impériale* and be called the *Pupilles de la Garde Impériale*;[5] but they were usually known as The King of Rome's Guard. At one time, they had a strength of 9,000, including children from Italy, Germany and Belgium.

Candidates had to be between ten and sixteen years of age and five feet or more in height, but moustaches were not compulsory![6]

5. The latin word *pupillus* means an orphan.
6. This is absolutely true.

VARIOUS UNITS

1. Conscrits Chasseurs
2. Fusilier, National Guard
3. Flanquers, Chasseurs
4. Training Battalion, Fontainebleau
5. Pupille
6. Officer's shako, Chasseurs
7. Officer's shako, Conscrits, Flanquers and Tirailleurs Chasseurs, Voltiguers and National Guard

8–11. Fusilier's shako, 1st–4th Companies National Guard

12. Shako, epaulette and sword-knot, Voltigeur of the National Guard
13. Shako, epaulette and sword-knot, Grenadier of the National Guard

8
9
10
11
12
13
1
2
3
4
5
6
7
L. & F.
FUNCKEN

At the First Restoration, the regiment was disbanded and most of the children returned home in preference to serving a new master.

Weapons and Colours

The colour illustrated, of which both faces are shown, belonged to the 2nd Regiment of *Grenadiers à Pied,* and that of the 1st Regiment was the same, except for the numeral. It was this latter colour that Napoleon kissed when he bade farewell at Fontainebleau. The staff, which was covered by a blue sleeve, was surmounted by a gilded brass eagle. The tricoloured silk sheet, of which the blue was to the hoist, was fringed with gold. The devices and the lettering were also in gold. The *cravate*[7] was tricoloured and fringed with gold.

The colour was carried by the 1st Battalion, and the 2nd Battalion had a plain red bunting flag, bearing in the centre and corners, a black grenade. This latter was mounted on a black staff which fitted into the muzzle of the musket of the non-commissioned officer who carried it. The Ensign's colour belt was of crimson decorated with gold.

Most of the weapons of the *Garde Impériale* were manufactured at Versailles under the supervision of one Boutet. Although of the same types as those carried by the regiments of the line, the weapons of the *Garde* were of superior workmanship. One of the most remarkable was the regulation pattern musket, over four feet, eight inches in length, and the carbine of the *Chasseurs à Cheval* with its bayonet nearly twenty inches in length. The officers' swords of various types were all masterpieces of workmanship, and are now much sought after by collectors.

7. The *cravate* is a broad ribbon tied in a bow at the head of the staff, immediately below the eagle.

DRUMMERS & DRUM-MAJORS (pp. 28-9)

1. Drum-Major, 3rd Grenadiers ('Ex-Hollandais'), full dress (1810–11)
2. Drum-Major, 1st Grenadiers
3. Drummers, Grenadiers
4. Drum-Major, 1st Grenadiers, full dress (1806)

WEAPONS & COLOURS

1 & 2. Obverse and reverse of the 2nd Grenadiers' colour (1812), 28″ square. That of the 1st Grenadiers was identical. It was carried with the blue to the hoist (pole), the staff was also blue

3. Sword, Grenadier Officer
4. Sword, Éclaireur
5. Sword, Grenadier
6. Sword, Officer of the Guard Infantry
7. Sword, Dragoon Officer
8. Sword, Lancers' Officer
9. Sword, Pioneer
10. Sword, Mameluke
11. Sword, Grenadier Officer
12. Cartridge-pouch, Grenadier Officer
13. Musket, Grenadiers
14. Carbine, Pioneer of the Guard

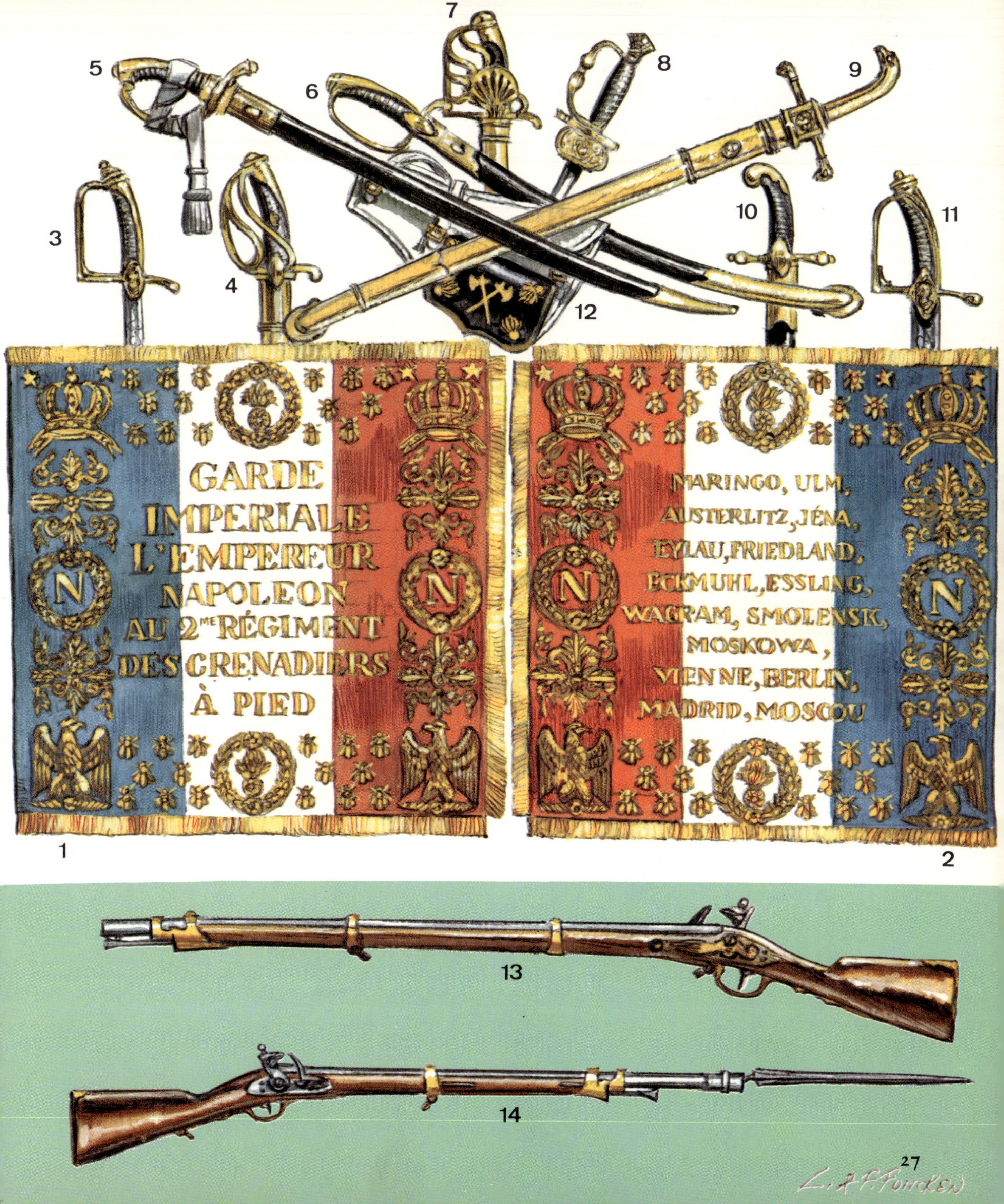
1
2
3
4
5
6
7
8
9
10
11
12
GARDE
IMPERIALE
L'EMPEREUR
NAPOLEON
AU 2ME RÉGIMENT
DES GRENADIERS
À PIED
N
MARINGO, ULM,
AUSTERLITZ, JÉNA,
EYLAU, FRIEDLAND,
ECKMUHL, ESSLING,
WAGRAM, SMOLENSK,
MOSKOWA,
VIENNE, BERLIN,
MADRID, MOSCOU
13
14
L. & F. FUNCKEN

1
2

3
4
L. & F. FUNCKEN

Bands and Drums

The musicians of the *Garde Impériale* were, if anything, even more striking in appearance than those of the infantry of the line.[8] The most astounding were the Drum-Majors, and here is how Louis Falloux describes them:

'Grenadier's coatee, trimmed along all seams with gold lace 1¼-inch wide having a toothed edge and ornamented with sequins; the collar, lapels, cuffs, free edges of the pocket-flaps and the turn-backs edged with the same lace; the button-holes on the lapels, the hip-buttons and the buttons on the pocket-flaps ornamented with loops with large bullion tassels; gold epaulettes with vellum lace straps and heavy bullions; on both forearms, the badges of rank of a serjeant-major.

'Waistcoat, with white gold lace.

'Breeches, white Hungarian pattern; gold lace stripes down the sides; gold laced and embroidered thigh ornaments in the form of an Hungarian knot.

'Black Hessian boots, trimmed and fringed in gold, for ordinary parades; the same, but in crimson leather, in review order.

'Black hat, trimmed with lace similar to that on the coatee 1½-inch wide and edged with red and white feathers; loop as for the officers, of lace ¾-in wide; large gold bullion tassels; white upright plume springing from a bunch of blue and red ostrich feathers.

'Belt, scarlet velvet, embroidered along the edges with gold oak-leaves, gold bullion trimming; on the front, a gold

8. See Volume I.

BANDSMEN

1 & 2. Bandsmen, 1st Grenadiers, full dress (1805–10)
3. Undress, winter (1808)
4. Negro Cymbalist, 1st Regiment (1805–10)
5. Bandsmen of the Dutch Grenadiers (1809–11)

Full dress was not worn after the Russian campaign

1
2
3
4
5

oak-leaf wreath, above which, a gold-embroidered grenade and a square gilt plate fitted with two miniature ebony drumsticks with ivory heads and connected by a silver chain; at the back, gold grenades.

'Sword, infantry officer's pattern; sword-knot with gold lace strap and bullion tassel; sword-belt, red, embroidered with gold oak-leaves.

'Staff with silver head decorated with gilt fasces and stars; silver ferrule; shaft criss-crossed with silver chain ending in two silver tassels.'[9]

By comparison, the dress of the other musicians was comparatively sober. The lapels, collar, cuffs and turn-backs were trimmed with vellum lace $\frac{3}{4}$-in wide, and the buttonhole loops had short tassels, all in gold. The hat was trimmed with gold and edged with red and white feathers. The sword-knot was of gold and red. In 1810, the lapels, collar, cuffs, cuff-slashes and turn-backs which were previously crimson, became scarlet. This was the only change made in the dress.

The drummers of the Grenadiers wore the same dress as the rank and file, but with gold and scarlet lace and wings. These last were discontinued in 1808. The drum-carriage was ornamented with a brass grenade and a square brass plate fitted with two miniature ebony, brass-mounted drumsticks. The drummers of the *Chasseurs à Pied* also wore the dress of the rank and file, but the lace was gold and green. On the drum-carriage, the grenade was replaced by a hunting horn.

9. *Garde Impériale* by Louis Falloux, published in 1901.

DRUMMERS

1. Pupille
2. Engineers
3. Légion de Gendarmerie d'Élite
4. Foot Artillery
5. Grenadiers ('Ex-Hollandais')
6. Marines

1
2
3
4
5
6
L. & F. Funcken

The Cavalry

Grenadiers à Cheval

The *Grenadiers à Cheval,* along with the *Grenadiers à Pied,* enjoyed the distinction of having fought at Marengo. Their terms of service were even more exclusive than those of the *Grenadiers à Pied.* On being transferred from the Consular Guard to the *Garde Impériale* on 29 July 1804, the regiment was organised with a Headquarters and four squadrons each of two troops, in all 1,018 men. On 15 April 1806, a squadron of *Vélites* was added to the establishment, and these men had to be not less than five feet, nine inches in height and to have a private income of 300 francs.

Under peace-time conditions, the *Vélites* were trained separately, and it was only on the march and in action that they served side by side with the Grenadiers. In war, the strength was increased to two regiments, each commanded by a major responsible to the colonel. Riding their traditional black horses, the *Grenadiers à Cheval* distinguished themselves in every battle right up to Waterloo.

The *Grenadiers à Cheval* wore the same coatees as the *Grenadiers à Pied.* Originally, they wore a golden yellow aiguillette on the right shoulder and a scale on the left; in 1807, a scale was added on the right. The bearskin had no plate. The jack-boots had soft legs in marching order, but in full dress, after 1802, ones with stiff legs were worn. On active service, the buckskin breeches were replaced by ones of cloth with leather strappings. For the officers, whatever was of golden yellow for the troops, was gold, both in the dress and in the horse furniture.

GRENADIERS À CHEVAL

1. Officer, full dress
2. Grenadier, full dress
3. Trumpeter

1
2
3
L & F. FUNCKEN

Chasseurs à Cheval

The *Chasseurs à Cheval* were formed from Napoleon's Guides, and they retained the latter's smart hussar uniform. Their establishment was the same as that of the *Grenadiers à Cheval*, but their *Vélites* were required only to have a minimum height of five feet and eight inches. The Guides of the Consular Guard were converted into *Chasseurs* on 29 July 1804, and were formed into four squadrons each of two troops.

The *Chasseurs à Cheval* were quartered in the *École Militaire* in Paris, and had the privilege of finding the squadron mounting guard on the Emperor's residence. On active service, this squadron acted as the Body Guard to Napolcon. The *Souvenirs du Capitaine Parquin, 1803-14* contain valuable information upon the subject:

'The squadron of *Chasseurs à Cheval* had certain special duties in connection with the Emperor. A Lieutenant, a sergeant, two corporals, twenty-two troopers and a trumpeter formed his escort. A corporal and four troopers, one of whom carried his papers and another his telescope, rode ahead and made way for him. If the Emperor dismounted, so did the *Chasseurs* who then fixed bayonets and marched with him. The officer commanding the escort kept always close to His Majesty and only Murat and Berthier were allowed to come close to him. When the Emperor moved into quarters, the officer commanding the escort occupied the room next to him. Two orderlies stood by, horses saddled, with a charger for the Emperor. They were relieved every two hours.'

The first person to see the Emperor when he left his quarters was the officer commanding the escort. It was a position of great trust. The escort, too, was devoted to the

CHASSEURS À CHEVAL I

1. Chasseur, full dress
2. 2nd Regiment (Young Guard), full dress (1815)
3. Trumpeter

2
1
3
L. & F. Funcken

Emperor and they were duly rewarded. Four men from each troop in both regiments of the Old Guard were given holdings along the canals or around Milan, which represented an income of anything from 500 to 800 francs, as well as the *Legion d'Honneur* and sometimes the Iron Crown with an annuity of 250 francs.

On 10 January 1813, the strength of the regiment was increased to eight squadrons each of 250 men and on 6 March following, a ninth squadron was added. The additional five squadrons were treated as part of the Young Guard and had their own uniform.

After his escape from Elba, Napoleon constituted the additional squadrons as the 2nd Regiment of *Chasseurs à Cheval* in the Young Guard, as a mark of his recognition.

The *Chasseurs à Cheval* were not confined in their duties to that of a Body Guard, and they frequently fought alongside the *Grenadiers à Cheval,* swards drawn, mounted on their bay or chestnut chargers.

Mamelukes

When Napoleon arrived in Egypt, the country was under despotic military rule.[10] On the return of the young *Général-en-Chef* to France, he formed a troop drawn from deserters from the service of Ibrahim Pasha and Murad Bey along with sundry Georgians, Armenians and Circassians who were fugitives from slavery. This motley crew made a very suitable escort for the future conqueror. When the *Garde Impériale* was set up in July 1804, Napoleon decreed that the Mameluke Troop would be attached to the *Chasseurs à Cheval.* It had a strength of 124 men, with a French Troop Headquarters. Between 1806 and 1810, its strength fell to 102 and then rose to 250 by January 1813, when it was re-formed as a squadron.

10. See *Arms and Uniforms II–18th Century to the Present Day.*

CHASSEURS À CHEVAL II

1. Picket, dismounted order, service dress
2. Busby
3. Pelisse
4. Jacket
5. Sword, Chasseur
6. Sword, Officer

2
3
4
5
6
1

We should mention that by no means all the 'Mamelukes' were really orientals. When they were disbanded in 1814, there were only eighteen true Mamelukes among them and they were massacred in Marseilles on their way home.

Roustan, Napoleon's Mameluke orderly, although heaped with honours by his master, deserted the Emperor when he was exiled to Elba, and put himself on show at fairs in London. He died in obscurity at Dourdan at the age of sixty-five. Contrary to popular belief, he was never one of the Mamelukes of the *Garde Impériale*.

The Mamelukes wore the tarbush (or fez) with a turban round the bottom, but changed to the cahouk, a similar but taller headdress in 1807. Over brightly-coloured shirts, they wore a waistcoat, and their baggy trousers were generally crimson, purple or scarlet. Their boots were red, green or yellow. They were mounted on the same breeds of charger as the *Chasseurs à Cheval,* not on arabs.

Chevau-légers Lanciers
1st Regiment (Polish Lancers)

At his entry into Warsaw in December 1806, Napoleon was escorted by a body guard of Polish Noblemen, and their splendour captured his imagination. In consequence, on 2 March 1807, he raised a regiment of Polish cavalry, four squadrons strong, that was to form part of the *Garde Impériale*. Any Pole, be he freed serf, nobleman or townsman, could enlist. The total establishment of the regiment, including the Headquarters, was 968 men and they were styled the *Chevau-légers Polonais*.

When they arrived in France, they were garrisoned at Chantilly. After the campaign of 1809, when the lance was adopted, the regiment was styled the *Chevau-légers Lanciers Polonais,* and commonly called the Polish Lancers.

MAMELUKES

1. Officer
2–3. Mamelukes
4. Standard-bearer

1
2
3
4
L. & F. FUNCKEN

It was at Wagram in 1809 that they made themselves into lancers by seizing the lances of the Austrian Uhlans, the better to chase them from the field of battle.

On 11 March 1812, a fifth squadron was raised and on 8 October in the same year, the strength of the regiment was increased to 1,500 men, but without any increase in the number of squadrons.

The Polish Lancers took part in many daring exploits. One, in particular, was at the Battle of Somosierra where one squadron put to flight 15,000 Spanish troops who were entrenched and had artillery support. Only fifteen Poles returned.

After the collapse in 1814, one hundred and twenty Polish Lancers accompanied Napoleon to Elba. During the Hundred Days, the survivors who had remained in France joined up with the Lancers from Elba to form a squadron, which was known by the old name of Polish Lancers, and they fought gallantly at Ligny. The Polish Lancers were always part of the Old Guard.

2nd Regiment

The 2nd Regiment was raised from the Hussars of the Dutch Guard of Louis Bonaparte on 13 September 1810 and brought up to strength with French troops. They became known as the Red Lancers.

On 10 January 1813, the regiment had eight squadrons each of 250 men. Then on 23 February, the squadron of Dragoons of the Paris Municipal Guard was incorporated, bringing the strength up to 2,500 men who were formed into ten squadrons. The first four squadrons were Dutch and formed part of the Middle Guard; the remainder were French and belonged to the Young Guard. During the Hundred Days, the regiment was reorganised and transferred to the Old Guard, under the name of the *Chevau-légers*

1st REGIMENT, POLISH LANCERS

1. Officer, full dress (1810–14)
2. Lancer, marching order (1812)
3. Lancer, full dress (1809–14)
4. Trumpeter, full dress (1807–14)

3
2
1
4

Lanciers de la Garde Impériale, and included the squadron of Polish Lancers.

The French element of the Red Lancers came mostly from Alsace and Lorraine. They distinguished themselves during the Russian Campaign and inflicted heavy casualties on the British Guards at Waterloo.

3rd Regiment

This regiment, which had a very short existence, was raised in Lithuania on 12 September 1812. Its uniform was the same as that of the 1st Regiment, except that the buttons were brass. This regiment was almost entirely destroyed at Slonim, in Russia, when the Colonel, General Konapka, a hero of the 1st Regiment during the Peninsular War, was wounded and taken prisoner.

Was there ever a 4th Regiment? Carle Vernet[11] made a drawing of a lancer of the 4th Regiment, which was included in an exhibition of his work in 1898, but the catalogue throws no further light on the matter.

Dragoons

A regiment of Dragoons was formed, on the lines of the *Grenadiers à Cheval,* on 15 April 1806. Their uniform was identical with that of the Grenadiers, except that it was green, instead of blue. The men were drawn from the dragoons of the line;[12] and had to be of good appearance, have at least ten years' service, and be not less than five feet, eight inches in height. The first time that she met the Regiment, during a review in the Place du Carrousel, the Empress decided that she would like to adopt it. Thenceforth, they were proud to be known as The Empress's Dragoons.

11. Carle Vernet (1758–1836) was a painter of battle, hunting scenes and of popular subjects. He is not a very reliable authority.

12. See Volume I.

2nd REGIMENT, CHEVAU-LÉGERS LANCIERS

1. Lancer, full dress (1811–14)
2. Undress (1811–14)
3. Young Guard, full dress
4. Officer, full dress (1811)
5. Trumpeter, full dress (1813)

4
5
1
2
3
L. & F. FUNCKEN

On the march, a squadron consisted of 200 Dragoons and 50 *Vélites,* so that the Regiment mustered 800 old soldiers and 200 youngsters between the four squadrons. At first the regiment rode blacks, but changed to chestnuts later.

At the First Restoration, the regiment became the *Corps Royal des Dragons de France* (The Royal Corps of French Dragoons), but it was re-established as part of the *Garde Impériale* upon Napoleon's return, on 8 April 1815. After the Capitulation of Paris, the regiment withdrew behind the Loire and was disbanded.

For many years afterwards, the survivors of the Empress's Dragoons held an annual reunion at Malmaison, on the anniversary of the death of the Empress Josephine.

Éclaireurs à Cheval

On 9 December 1813, three regiments of *Éclaireurs à Cheval* were raised for service in the *Garde Impériale,* each consisting of four squadrons of 250 men each. The 1st and 2nd Regiments were drawn from conscripts and from the cavalry of the line, and the 3rd Regiment from the Poles. The three Regiments were attached respectively to the *Grenadiers à Cheval,* to the Dragoons and to the Polish Lancers.

The first two Regiments were divided equally between the Old Guard and the Young Guard. The 3rd Regiment, whose uniform is not shown, wore the dress of the Polish Lancers, but had white pompoms without any plume, blue and white striped girdle and a plain blue shabracque.

Impetuous and courageous, these men were never actually employed as scouts (*éclaireur*). In 1814, the first two Regiments were transferred to the line, and the third sent back to Poland.

Half the *Éclaireurs* were armed with the lance carrying a crimson and white pennon, and half with the carbine. All were armed with two pistols and a sword with a brass hilt and a steel scabbard with brass mountings.

DRAGOONS

1. Dragoon, service dress (1806)
2. Full dress (1806)
3. Turnback
4. Helmet, other ranks
5. Officer's helmet. The peak was sometimes covered with fur, as for the other ranks

4
5
1
2
3
L. & F. Funcken

The Gendarmes d'Élite and Gendarmes d'Ordonnance

Gendarmes d'Élite

The *Légion de Gendarmerie d'Élite* was formed to provide guards for palaces and headquarters, and was raised on 29 July 1804, with a Headquarters, two squadrons of two troops each, and a half-battalion of two companies of foot, a total strength of 632 gendarmes. After 1806, there remained only the two mounted squadrons with a strength of 456 men. They rode blacks.

Their duties consisted of:

1. Two mounted guards, one at the Tuileries and one at Malmaison, who had to find despatch riders and escorts for the Emperor's carriage;

2. A dismounted sentry on the terrace of the Tuileries beside the public gardens; and

3. Two sentries at the prison at *La Tour du Temple*.

Outside their ordinary duties, the *Gendarmerie d'Élite* were responsible for matters of security such as finding an escort for the Pope or for Processions of the Blessed Sacrament. Likewise, they were responsible for the security of the Emperor and his suite when they travelled.

On active service, the Gendarmes fought alongside the Cavalry of the *Garde Impériale*. They also had to guard prisoners of war and trophies which were waiting to be handed over to the Emperor.

Up to 1806, the dismounted branch were only distinguishable from the mounted branch by their black leggings, their grenadier epaulettes without aiguillettes, the absence of a festoon on the red-plumed bearskin and their equipment which was the same as for the *Gendarmerie à Pied*.[13]

13. See Volume I.

ÉCLAIREURS

1. Éclaireur, 2nd Regiment (1813)
2. 1st Regiment, full dress (1813)
3. 1st Regiment (Young Guard 1813)

3
2
1
L. & F. FUNCKEN

Gendarmes d'Ordonnance

In 1806, Napoleon opened the ranks of the *Garde Impériale* to the returned *émigrés*. All the same, they had to dress, equip, and mount themselves at their own expense, and find their own way to Mayence (Mainz). The arrival of these expensive aristocrats was resented by the Army. The first three troops acquitted themselves in battle, but no more, and the fourth troop reached Germany just in time for the disbandment of the Corps on 12 July 1807.

A company of foot also existed in theory, and this was disbanded in April 1807 for lack of recruits because the well-to-do volunteers preferred to be mounted.

The Lanciers de Berg and the Lithuanian Tartars

On 17 December 1809, Napoleon added yet another regiment to the *Garde Impériale*, the *Chevau-légers de Berg*, which had been raised in 1807 by Murat, Duke of Berg.[14] After their transfer, they were armed with the lance and became

14. The *Chevau-légers de Berg* will be covered with the other German allied armies.

GENDARMES D'ÉLITE & D'ORDONNANCE

1. Gendarme d'Élite, full dress
2. Rear view of same
3. Trumpeter
4. Gendarme d'Ordonnance (1806–7)

4
1
2
3
L.-A F. FUNCKEN

known as the *Lanciers de Berg*. They were trained in the use of the lance by the non-commissioned officers of the Polish lancers, and they fought, with heavy losses, in the Peninsular War pursuing the guerillas and in battle against the British, including the King's German Legion.[15] On their return from Spain, they took part in the disastrous Russian Campaign, in which they were formed into two regiments, the 1st and 2nd *Chevau-légers de Berg*. They were practically annihilated at Borissow, but the survivors fought on in Germany, where they finally disappeared.

On 24 August 1812, a troop of Lithuanian Tartars was attached to the Polish Lancers. These were the remains of a squadron raised in Lithuania from the Mahommedan nobles descended from the Tartar families that had settled there in the Middle Ages. They were used as scouts. They were practically wiped out in Russia, and the survivors went to the 3rd *Éclaireurs* at the end of 1813. After Napoleon's abdication, the remaining Tartars went back to Lithuania.

The Artillery and the Engineers

Foot Artillery

By a decree dated 7 April 1808, four companies of Foot Artillery were added to the *Garde Impériale*. These were increased to eight in 1810 and to nine in 1812, all organised as a single regiment. In the following year, a second regiment was raised, and this was attached to the Young Guard. In 1814, the Foot Artillery of the *Garde Impériale* was transferred to the line, but it was re-formed with a strength of six companies in 1815.

15. See Volume I.

LANCIERS DE BERG & LITHUANIAN TARTARS

1. Lanciers de Berg, Light Troop (1813)
2. Lithuanian Tartar (1813)

2
1
L. & F. FUNCKEN

Men with six years' service in the artillery of the line of a height of not less than five feet, nine inches, were eligible to transfer to the Foot Artillery of the *Garde Impériale*.

Horse Artillery

The Horse Artillery was added to the *Garde Impériale* on 29 July 1804, when an extra troop was added to the one that had been in the Consular Guard. Each troop was 98 men strong. In April 1806, a regiment of three squadrons, each of two troops, was formed. Each squadron consisted of 100 old soldiers and 20 *Vélites*. On the introduction of the Foot Artillery into the *Garde Impériale*, the Horse Regiment was reduced to four troops. The artillery of the *Garde Impériale* consisted of 198 pieces, formed into 26 batteries. The conditions of entry were eight years' previous service and a height of not less than five feet and nine inches.

Artillery Train

In 1806, the Artillery Train consisted of a battalion of six companies and it had increased to eight companies by 1812. Upon Napoleon's return, it was reorganised into one squadron of eight troops.

Engineers

The Engineer Company of the *Garde Impériale* was raised on 16 July 1810. Its duties were to act as a Fire Brigade in the Imperial palaces. This came about because the guard at Saint-Cloud, where the Emperor was staying at the time, set fire to one of the rooms by allowing a stove to overheat. To prevent any repetition of this, Napoleon had special night guards mounted at all the Imperial residences.

The Engineer Company had a strength of 250 men in 1813. By the next year, it had been formed into a battalion, 400 strong of all ranks. It was disbanded when Napoleon abdicated, and re-formed as a company of 200 men on his return.

ARTILLERY & ENGINEERS

1. Horse Artillery, full dress (1805)
2. Horse Artillery, marching order (1806–7)

3 & 4. Foot Artillery
5 & 6. Engineers (1810)
7 & 8. Artillery Train

1
2
3
4
5
6
7
8
L. & F. FUNCKEN

The Marines

Marines

On 17 September 1803, a naval battalion was added to the Consular Guard. This consisted of a headquarters and five divisions. For the most part, the men came from the South of France and Corsica. In each battalion, one third of the men carried cutlasses, one third had boarding-axes and one third had pikes. Every man had two pistols at the waist. It is probable that they did not receive muskets until they were brought into the *Garde Impériale* on 29 July 1804.

The Marines were raised primarily for service in the ships that were destined to carry Napoleon and his staff to England and when the Grand Army[16] was withdrawn from the Channel Coast, the Marines went too. They took part in the Austrian Campaign in 1805, in the role of Inland Water Transport troops, conveying food, ammunition and artillery, which would have been extremely difficult by road. They were present at the Capitulation of Ulm[17] on 20 October 1805, and later at the Battle of Austerlitz, but they took no part. The Marines returned to Paris in 1806.

On 16 September 1810, the establishment of the Marines of the *Garde Impériale* was fixed at 1,136 men, organised in six companies, to which two more were added in 1811. They were disbanded at Fontainebleau in April 1814, but a detachment of 35 accompanied the Emperor in his exile.

During the Hundred Days, the Marines of the *Garde* were resuscitated, but consisted of a single division of 150 men. After playing an active part in the defence of Paris, the Marines were withdrawn behind the Loire, and finally disbanded. Although few in number, the Marines played their part in achieving Napoleon's victories.

16. See Volume I.

17. See the section on the Austrian army below.

MARINES

1. Full dress (1810)
2. Service dress with *caraco* (jacket)
3. Officer (1807)
4. Service dress (1806–13)
5. Trumpeter (1807)

2
3
4
1
5

The Gardes d'Honneur

After the Russian Campaign in which Napoleon lost countless men and horses, he realised that the Allies might try to finish him off once and for all, should the opportunity present itself. Accordingly, every section of society was called upon to help re-form the Imperial Army. Up to now, the nobility and the upper middle classes had found replacements to serve in the place of their sons. Napoleon decided to turn the tables on these defaulters and to tempt them to take service by holding out a gaudy uniform, which was to be bought at their own expense, and the honour of joining his personal body guard.

By hook or by crook, four regiments were formed by raking in Dutchmen, Italians and Belgians. Indeed, a quarter of the men in the 1st and 2nd Regiments were Belgians. Like the *Gendarmes d'Ordonnance*, the *Gardes d'Honneur* were resented by the rest of the *Garde Impériale*, but they made good by their gallant conduct. They became part of the *Garde* on 29 July 1813; the 1st Regiment was attached to the *Chasseurs à Cheval*, the 2nd to the Dragoons, the 3rd to the *Grenadiers à Cheval*, and the 4th Regiment to the Lancers.

Still not very firm in the saddle, the *Gardes d'Honneur* charged the Russians at Hanau in 1813. In March 1814, although no longer part of the *Garde Impériale*, they gained the acclamation of the Grenadiers when they charged the Russians at Rheims. True to their oath, they fought for the 'Corsican Adventurer' under the walls of Paris as long as he was free.

GARDES D'HONNEUR

1. Officer
2. Trooper
3. Trumpeter
4. Shakoes of 1st to 4th Companies

1
2
3
4
L. & F. FUNCKEN

THE ALLIES OF THE FRENCH

Bavaria

Maximilian Joseph, Elector of Bavaria, had made an alliance with Napoleon in 1805. On 12 July 1806 accordingly, Bavaria joined the Confederation of the Rhine with a contingent of 30,000 men.

Infantry of the Line

The Infantry of the Line wore bright blue coatees. Between 1800 and 1806, there were the following regiments:

Regiment	Collar, Lapels and Cuffs[18]	Buttons
Leibregiment	Black (red in 1802)	White metal
Kurprinz	Black (red in 1802)	Brass
Herzog Carl	Red	
Weichs	Pale Yellow	White metal
Preysing	Pink with red piping	White metal
Herzog Wilhelm	Red	White metal
Morawitzky	White	Brass
Herzog Pius	Pale Yellow	Brass
Isenburg	Scarlet	Brass
Junker	Crimson	White metal

In 1811, there were twelve regiments:

18. See annotated diagrams in Volume I.

Regiment	Lapels and Cuffs	Collar	Piping	Buttons
1st König	Poppy	Poppy		White metal
2nd Kronprinz	Poppy	Poppy		Brass
3rd Prinz Carl	Poppy	Poppy	White	Brass
4th Sacheen-Hildburghausen	Yellow	Yellow	Poppy	White metal
5th Preysing	Pink	Pink		White metal
6th Herzog Wilhelm	Poppy	Poppy	White	White metal
7th Lowenstein Wertheim	Pink	Pink		Brass
8th Herzog Pius	Yellow	Yellow	Poppy	Brass
9th Isenburg	Yellow	Poppy	Poppy	Brass
10th Junker	Yellow	Poppy	Poppy	White metal
11th Kinkel	Black	Poppy	Poppy	White metal
12th	*Disbanded for indiscipline*			
13th (no name)	Black	Poppy	Poppy	Brass

The 1st and 2nd Regiments had button-holes matching the buttons on the lapels and cuffs.

Light Infantry

In 1806, the light infantry consisted of six battalions dressed in bright green at first, but later in dark green.

Battalion	Lapels and Cuffs	Collar	Piping	Buttons
1	Black	Poppy	Poppy	Yellow
2	Black	Poppy	Poppy	White
3	Black	Black	Poppy	White
4	Black	Black	Poppy	Yellow
5	Crimson	Crimson	Poppy	White
6	Crimson	Crimson	Poppy	Yellow

On 29 April 1811, these battalions were re-organised and their uniforms were altered. The lapels and cuffs became black with poppy piping, and the collars and buttons were as follows:

Battalion	Collar	Buttons
1. Gedoni	Poppy	Brass
2. Wrede	Poppy	White metal
3. Berclau	Black	White metal
4. Theobald	Black	Brass
5. Buttler	Yellow	White metal
6. La Roche	Yellow	Brass

Dragoons and Chevau-légers

Between 1806 and 1811, there were two regiments of Dragoons and four regiments of *Chevau-légers*. The Dragoons wore white coatees with black facings and a stripe of the distinguishing colour on the turnbacks. In 1807, the facings were changed to red and then in 1811, the Dragoons were converted into the 1st and 2nd Regiments of *Chevau-légers*, bringing the total to six. The distinguishing colours were:

Regiment	Lapels, Cuffs and Stripe on Turnbacks	Collar	Piping	Buttons
1 (No name)	Poppy	Green		White metal
2 Taxis	Poppy	Green		Brass
3 Kronprinz	Black	Black	Poppy	Brass
4 König	Poppy	Poppy		White metal
5 Leiningen	Poppy	Poppy		Brass
6 Bubenhofen	Black	Black		White metal

Hussars

In December 1813, the *Land-Husarenkorps* was raised on a territorial basis and, in 1815, it was re-formed into two Line regiments. The only visible distinction between them was that the 1st Regiment wore black shakos, and the 2nd Regiment red ones.

Uhlans

In 1813, a regiment of Uhlans, dressed like the Austrian Uhlans, was raised. Their facings were originally light blue, but were changed to red in 1814.

Artillery

When Bavaria joined the Confederation of the Rhine, the Artillery adopted the coatee. Their only distinguishing mark was a pistol carried in a holster on a shoulder belt. Bavaria deserted the Confederation on 8 October 1813, and joined the Allies on the eve of the Battle of Leipzig.

BAVARIA–INFANTRY OF THE LINE

1. Grenadier, 4th Regiment (1806)
2. 2nd Regiment (1806)
3. N.C.O., 11th Regiment (1810)
4. Bavarian musket
5. Infantry helmet (1809)
6. Grenadier helmet (1806)

4
1
2
3
5
6

Würtemberg

Württemberg joined the Confederation of the Rhine on 12 July 1806 and so committed herself to finding a contingent of 12,000 men for Napoleon.

Four years earlier, Frederick, Duke of Württemberg, had signed a treaty with France by which he received nine cities belonging to the Holy Roman Empire and eight Ecclesiastical Territories, in exchange for the land that he surrendered on the West Bank of the Rhine. Having been raised to the rank of an Elector in 1803, Frederick then had to provide troops for the Austrian Campaign of 1805. After Austerlitz, he was rewarded by being proclaimed King on 1 January 1806.

As a result of joining the Confederation, Württemberg had doubled her area by 1810. Naturally, however, there had to be give and take and people of the country had to find troops for the Emperor to fight in some of his bloodiest campaigns.

It is only fair to say that the Württemberg government, following France, introduced important changes in the application of the law, freedom of religion and a more even justice.

Bavaria, whom we mentioned in the last chapter, gained similar advantages from her alliance with France. Having annexed numerous Ecclesiastical Territories and seventeen cities, she further enriched herself with the Margraviate of Burgau, the Principality of Eichstätt, the Vorarlberg, the Tyrol and so on. Nevertheless, after Napoleon's defeat at Leipzig where, between 15 and 19 October 1813, half a million men were engaged, Frederick I came over to the Allies.

BAVARIA–CAVALRY & ARTILLERY (pp. 66–7)

1. 5th Regiment, Chevau-légers (1807)
2. 1st Dragoons (1807)
3. Garde du Corps (1814)
4. Uhlan (1814), when formed in 1813 they had bright blue facings
5. Ammunition waggon with forage and team
6. 7th Regiment, Chevau-légers (1813)
7. Gun and limber
8. Volunteer, Hussar (1813–14)

BAVARIA

1 & 2. Private and N.C.O., Grenadiers of the Guard (1814)

3. Light Infantry (1805)
4. Light Infantry (1812)

5 & 6. Gunners (1808–11)

7. Drummer, Infantry of the Line (1807)
8. Driver, Artillery Train (1812)

3
4
5
6
1
2
7
8
L. & F. Funcken

6
5
1
2

8
7
4
3
L. & F. FUNCKEN .68

By the Treaty of Fulda, signed on 2 November 1813, the Austrians, the Prussians and the Russians recognised Frederick I's sovereignty over the new Württemberg, but the Congress of Vienna was to take a different view.

When Württemberg came in with France, there were eight regiments of Infantry of the Line, two of Light Infantry and four of Cavalry, together with the Artillery and the Royal Guard.

Infantry of the Line

The Infantry of the Line wore blue coatees with the collar, cuffs, turnbacks, shoulder-straps and half-lapels either in the distinguishing colour or the same as the body of the garment.

Regiment	Collar, Cuffs & Turnbacks	Half Lapels & Shoulder Straps
1	Yellow	Yellow
2	Sky Blue piped with white	Sky Blue piped with white
3	Red	Red
4	Red	Blue piped with red
5	White piped with red	White piped with red
6	White piped with red	White piped with red
7	Yellow	Blue piped with yellow
8	Pink piped with white	Pink piped with white

In 1812, half-lapels in the distinguishing colour were replaced by ones of the colour of the coatee, piped with white.

Regiment	Collar, Cuffs and Shoulder-Straps	Turnbacks
1	Yellow piped with white	Yellow
2	Sky Blue piped with white	Sky Blue
3	Orange-Red piped with white	Orange-Red
4	Black piped with white	Black
5	White piped with red	White
6	White piped with red	White
7	Yellow piped with white	Yellow
8	Red piped with white	Yellow

WÜRTTEMBURG–INFANTRY

1. 1st Regiment (1806)
2. 8th Regiment (1806)
3. Chasseur à Pied (1806)
4. 1st Leibregiment (1813)

1
2
3
4
L. & F. Funcken

In 1813, point-cuffs and shakos were adopted and the following distinctive colours were taken into use:

Regiment	Collar and Cuffs (with white lace and buttonholes)	Turnbacks	Piping
1	Yellow	Yellow	White
2	Sky Blue (ordinary cuffs)	Sky blue	White
3	Orange-Red	Orange-Red	White
4	Black (ordinary cuffs, no buttonholes)	Black	White
5	White	White	Red
6	White	White	Red
7	Yellow	Yellow	Yellow
8	Pink (no buttonholes)	Pink	White

Chasseurs

In 1805, there were two battalions of *Chasseurs*, who wore the traditional green coatee with black facings.[19] In 1807, the lapels became green and the 1st Battalion was distinguished by yellow button-holes and brass buttons on the collar and cuffs, while the 2nd Battalion retained white metal buttons.

Light Infantry

In 1805, there were two battalions of light infantry: the 1st Battalion was called successively de Neubronn (1805), then Bünau and finally Wolff (1807); the 2nd Battalion was de Scheler (1805), Brüsselle (1806) and Stockmayer (1813). The uniform was the same as that of the infantry, but dark green with sky blue as the distinguishing colour. The crested helmet was replaced by the shako in 1807.

Cavalry

The Württemberg cavalry consisted of *Chevau-légers*, *Chasseurs à Cheval*, Dragoons and *Uhlans* (lancers). These last were only introduced in 1815.

19. See the different chapters on *Chasseurs* in Volume I.

WÜRTTEMBURG

1 & 2. 58th Light Infantry (1805 and 1807), note the folding bayonet
3. 57th Regiment (1814)
4. 58th Regiment (1814)
5. Royal Foot Guards (1806)
6. Grenadier, Royal Foot Guards (1808–13)
7. Chasseur, Royal Foot Guard (1809–13)
8. Drum-Major, 4th Regiment (1811)
9. Cornet-player, 5th Chasseurs (1807)
10. Officer, Fusiliers (1808)

1
2
3
4
5
6
7
8
9
10
L. & F. FUNCKEN

WÜRTTEMBURG–CAVALRY & ARTILLERY

1. Chasseur à Cheval, Duke Henry's Regiment (1811)
2. Chasseur à Cheval, Prince Adam's Regiment (late Duke Henry's, 1813)
3. Gunner, Foot Artillery of the Guard (1813)
4. Gunner, Horse Artillery of the Guard (1807)
5. Chasseur à Cheval, Duke Louis's Regiment (1805)

The following were the distinguishing colours in 1806:

Regiments	Jacket	Collar	Lapels	Cuffs	Turnbacks	Breeches	Buttons
Duke Henri's Chevau-lègers	Blue	Red	Red	Red	Red	White	Brass
Leit-Chevau-lègers	Blue	Red	Blue	Red	Yellow	White	White
Prince Adam's Chevau-lègers (1811–12)	Blue	Yellow	Blue	Yellow	Yellow	White	White
Duke Louis's Chasseurs à Cheval	Green	Yellow	Green	Green	Yellow	Green	White
The King's Chasseurs à Cheval	Green	Green	Pink	Green	Green	White	White
Duke Louis's Regiment	Green	Green	Green	Green	Yellow	Green	White
The Crown Prince's Dragoons	Green	White	Green	Green	White	White	White
Garde du Corps	Yellow	Black		Black		White	White
Chasseurs of the Guard (1809)	Green	Black		Black	Yellow	White	Brass
Grenadiers à Cheval 1st and 2nd Squadron	Blue	Yellow				White	White
Guides (Leib-Jäeger)	Green	Red	Red	Red	Yellow	White	Brass

In addition to the mounted regiments of the Guard, there was also a battalion of *Leib-grenadiers,* composed of Fusiliers and Grenadiers. Finally, there were the *Chasseurs* of the Guard.

The Artillery was also divided between the Guard and the Line, the former being distinguished by white button-holes on their uniforms.

6. Gunner, Horse Artillery, The King's Household
7. Guide (1806)
8. Dragoon, Crown Prince's Regiment (1809)
9. Guide (1807)
10. Chasseur à Cheval, Garde du Corps (1809)
11. Leib-Chevau-légers (1805)
12. Gunner, Horse Artillery of the Guard (1813)

1
2
3
4
5
6
7
8
9
10
11
12
L. & F. FUNCKEN

Hesse-Darmstadt

Like his partners in the Confederation of the Rhine, Louis X, Landgrave of Hesse, had also considerably extended his possessions and had assumed the title of Grand Duke Louis I of Hesse. He did not desert Napoleon until November 1813.

Infantry
The three infantry units that existed before 1806 were gradually developed into three regiments clothed and equipped after the French fashion. Each was divided into two battalions of one grenadier company, one Light Infantry company and four Line companies each. However only the Crown Prince's Regiment was brought up to full strength, while the other two consisted of four Line companies each. All wore blue coatees with white button-holes.

Regiment	Collar, Lapels and Cuffs	Cuff Slashes	Turnbacks	Buttons
Guards Regiment	Red	as coat	Red	White metal
Leibregiment	Light Blue	Light Blue	Red	White metal
Crown Prince's Regiment	Yellow	as coat	Red	White metal

In 1813, the white button-holes were discontinued except on the lapels. At this time, there was also a short-lived regiment of Light Infantry, who had scarlet facings and white metal-buttons.

Cavalry
The cavalry consisted of the *Garde du Corps*, Hussars and *Chevau-légers*. They were distinguished as follows:

Garde du Corps: pale yellow coatee with red collar and cuffs, the latter laced with white; turn-backs pale yellow; buckskin breeches; black hat with a plume crimson over white.

WÜRTTEMBURG–ROYAL CAVALRY

1. Guide in surcoat (1808)
2. Garde du Corps in surcoat (1807). Although this looked like a cuirass, it was made of cloth
3. Horse Grenadier, Garde du Corps (1808)

1
2
3
L. & F. FUNCKEN

Hussars (disbanded in 1806): white shako with black plume; white jacket and light blue pelisse, laced and braided in white; light blue breeches; Hungarian boots.

Chevau-légers: dark green coatee, red collar with a black tab, black lapels and cuffs; white breeches or grey overalls; Roman-style helmet with a curiously-shaped frontal.

Artillery

The Artillery wore a uniform similar to that of the infantry, but of a darker blue.

The Hessians fought in the Peninsular War.

Westphalia

When Westphalia joined the Confederation of the Rhine in November 1807, apart from veteran companies and local defence units, her army consisted of eight regiments of Infantry of the Line, four of Light Infantry, the Foot Guards composed of three battalions of Grenadiers, *Chasseurs* and *Elite Jäeger Carabinier*.

The Cavalry consisted of two regiments of *Chevau-légers*, two of Cuirassiers and two of Hussars, together with the *Gendarmerie*. There was also a squadron of the *Garde du Corps* and three squadrons of *Chevau-légers Lanciers*. Including the Artillery, the army had a strength of 25,000 men.

It should be remembered that the Kingdom of Westphalia was created by Napoleon for his brother Jerome Bonaparte. Her territory had been greatly extended by the annexation of lands belonging to Hanover, Prussia and Hesse.

HESSE-DARMSTADT–INFANTRY

1. Musketeer, Foot Guards (1803–7)
2. Grenadier, Crown Prince's Regiment (1809)
3. Leib-regiment

1
2
3
L. & F. FUNCKEN

Infantry of the Line

The uniform of the infantry of the line was white; the eight regiments were distinguished by the colour of the collar, lapels, cuffs and cuff-slashes, and the linings. The 1st and 2nd Regiments had dark blue, the 3rd and 4th Regiments had light blue, the 5th and 6th Regiments had yellow and the 7th and 8th Regiments had dark blue originally, then black.

In 1810, the uniform was modified and the distinctive colours disappeared. A white coatee with square lapels appeared, this had the lapels, collar, cuffs and cuff-slashes of dark blue piped with white, and the turnbacks in white piped with dark blue.

Light Infantry

Originally, the Light Infantry wore cornflower blue with orange facings, but this was changed to dark green with light blue facings, the breeches also being dark green. All the infantry were armed and equipped by the French.

Cavalry

● Chevau-légers

The 1st Regiment, raised in 1808, wore dark green coatees with orange facings. They were originally armed with carbines, but adopted the lance in 1811. The 2nd *Chevau-légers Lanciers* were raised in October 1812, but seem to have existed only on paper. Their facings would have been buff.

● Cuirassiers

Two regiments were formed, one in 1808 and the second in 1811. The 1st Regiment had a white coatee with rose facings, and the 2nd Regiment a dark blue coatee with orange facings. Both Regiments had scarlet epaulettes and white metal buttons. The 1st Regiment wore only the front plate of the cuirass, but the 2nd Regiment wore both the front and back plates.

HESSE-DARMSTADT–CAVALRY

1. Garde du Corps (1805–15)
2. Chevau-léger (1810–15)

1
2
L. & F. FUNCKEN

● Hussars

The Hussars wore French-style uniforms. The 1st Regiment wore dark green with facings of the same colour, and the 2nd Regiment wore light blue with red facings. In both Regiments the lace and braid were white, the buttons were white metal and the fur on the pelisse was black.

Foot Guards

● Grenadiers

The Grenadiers wore white, long-skirted coatees with red facings and yellow button-holes on the collar, lapels and cuffs, and yellow grenades on the turnbacks. On the march, they wore grey or yellowish overalls over their grey leggings. The officers wore a similar uniform, but with gold-lace button-holes with little tassels, their epaulettes were gold instead of red.

● Chasseurs

The Chasseurs wore a uniform of the same cut as that of the Grenadiers, but in green with yellow piping, collars and cuffs. The button-holes were white. The breeches were green with thigh ornaments in the form of Hungarian knots like those of the Hussars. The skirt-ornaments were in the form of hunting horns.[20] The officers' uniforms were laced with silver.

● Elite Jäeger Carabiniers

This regiment wore a green, single-breasted coatee with brass buttons. The facings were green piped with red, except for the collar. The thigh ornaments in the form of Hungarian knots were red. The epaulettes were green with red fringes.

20. This was the usual badge for *Chasseurs* (see Volume I).

WESTPHALIA–CAVALRY

1. Chevau-lèger Lancier of the Guard (1812)
2. Cuirassier, 2nd Regiment (1812)
3. 1st Hussars (1812)

1
2
3
L. & F. FUNCKEN

Garde du Corps

The *Garde du Corps,* which consisted of one squadron, was raised in 1808. They wore a dark blue coatee which fastened with seven brass buttons on the right. The collar and cuffs were red with yellow button-holes, the turnbacks were red with yellow grenades. White breeches were worn in summer, blue in winter. Yellow aiguillettes were worn on the right side. Only the front plate of the cuirass was worn, and this was secured by cross straps at the back. The elaborate helmet had a white metal plate with the Royal Cypher in brass and the same device ensigned with the Crown appeared on the hilt of the sword. The full dress was white with blue facings, red piping and gold-laced button-holes.

Chevau-légers of the Guard

This regiment wore dark green, short-skirted coatees with scarlet facings and yellow button-holes on the collar, cuffs and lapels. The breeches were green with yellow Hungarian-knot thigh ornaments and were covered with green overalls with black strappings and scarlet stripes on service. Originally, the Regiment carried the sword and the pistol but, in 1811, they adopted the lance like their counterparts in the line. Accordingly they were re-named *Chevau-légers Lanciers* of the Guard.

Hussars of the Guard

The King of Württemberg had in his pay a regiment of Hussars known as Jerome Napoleon's Hussars. When the Kingdom of Württemberg collapsed, Napoleon disbanded the regiment, but, at his brother's request, brought them on to the strength of the French Army as the 13th Hussars.

WESTPHALIA–ROYAL GUARDS

1. Hussar, 1st Regiment (Jerome-Napoleon, 1813)
2. King Jerome's Garde du Corps (1812), he is wearing a half-cuirass secured by crossed straps decorated with brass scales

L. & F. FUNCKEN

They wore a red jacket with blue cuffs, a blue pelisse trimmed with white fur, blue breeches, and a red shako. The lace and braid was yellow. The valise was blue with yellow lace. The regiment was practically decimated at Fère-Champenoise on 25 March 1814.

Artillery

The Foot Artillery wore the same uniform as the infantry but in dark blue with red facings and epaulettes. The breeches were blue and the leggings were black. In summer, on the march or in action, the gunners wore yellowish-grey overalls and various coloured leggings. The shako-cover was painted with a yellow grenade in front.

The Artillery of the Guard wore a similar uniform, but the coatee was 'fly-away' and was worn over a red waistcoat braided in yellow. There was a yellow aiguillette on the left shoulder.

Mecklenburg–Würtzburg–Lippe–Schwartzburg

The Duchy of Mecklenburg-Schwerin joined the Confederation of the Rhine on 24 April 1808 and provided a contingent of two battalions of six companies and a company of artillery, with a total strength of 1,900 men. The artillery wore the same uniform as the infantry, but with black

WESTPHALIA–FOOT GUARDS

1. Elite Jäeger Carabinier (1812)
2 & 3. Grenadiers of the Guard (1812)
4. Drummer, Grenadiers of the Guard (1808)
5. Chasseur of the Guard (1812)

1
2
3
4
5
L. & F.

facings. Mecklenburg-Strelitz wore the same uniform, but with brass buttons. They supplied 400 men who were amalgamated with those from Schwerin to form the 7th Confederation Regiment.

The Grand Duchy of Würtzburg found a regiment of infantry and one of cavalry, together with some artillery, which were taken on the strength on 30 September 1806.

The Principalities of Lippe-Detmold and Schaumburg-Lippe joined the Confederation on 18 April 1807, and found contingents of 500 and 150 men respectively, which, with the Anhalt Battalion,[21] formed the 5th Confederation Regiment. Both contingents wore the same dress.

The Principalities of Schwartzburg-Sonderhausen and Schwartzburg-Rudolstadt joined the Confederation on 13 April 1807, and undertook each to find 325 men. Together, these formed one battalion of four companies. They were combined with the troops from Waldeck and from Reuss to make up the 6th Confederation Regiment. The four Schwartzburg companies wore the same uniform.

Cleve-Berg–Nassau–Baden

The Grand Duchy of Cleve-Berg, which had been overrun by the French revolutionary armies, was given by Napoleon to Murat in 1806, and joined the Confederation on 12 July of that year. Her contribution was fixed at 5,000 men to be made up of four infantry regiments, one cavalry regiment, five artillery companies and an engineer detachment to include sappers, miners and bridgers. These last, who were volunteers, served with the French troops.

21. For Anhalt, see under Waldeck.

WESTPHALIA

1. Grenadier (1807)
2. Voltigeur (1812)
3. Officer
4. Fusilier
5. Grenadier, full dress, summer
6. Light Infantry

3
1
2
4
5
6

The Principalities of Nassau-Usingen and Nassau-Weilburg joined the Confederation in 1806 and, along with Hohenzollern, Salm, Isenburg, Liechtenstein and Arenberg, found 4,000 men. In 1809, Nassau raised two infantry regiments who wore green coatees, grey breeches and yellow equipment which was peculiar to them. There was also a regiment of *Chasseurs à Cheval* of two squadrons of 125 men each, they were volunteers and mostly well-to-do. The Nassau troops were engaged mostly in Spain, where the 2nd Infantry Regiment, almost to a man and including the Colonel, went over to the British. The remainder were disarmed and put in prison in Normandy until Napoleon's fall.

The Grand Duchy of Baden joined the Confederation in July 1806, and had to provide 8,000 men who made up four infantry regiments, two cavalry regiments, one battalion of rifles, and an element of Horse and Foot Artillery.

In 1806, the uniforms of the infantry were as follows:

WÜRTZBURG

1. Grenadier (1807)
2. Grenadier (1812)
3. Dragoon (Chevau-lèger, 1807)
4. Dragoon (Chevau-lèger, 1812)
5. Gunner (1812)

MECKLENBURG

6. Grenadier (1808)

SCHWARTZBURG

7. Private, Infantry
8. Officer, Infantry (1810)

LIPPE

9. Officer, Infantry (1808)
10. Private, (Infantry 1812)

Regiment	Jacket	Collars and Cuffs	Turnbacks	Breeches	Buttons
Grenadiers of the Guard	Blue	Red	Red	White	White metal
Infantry of the Line	Blue	Red	Red	White	White metal
Chasseurs	Green	Black	Black	Grey	White metal
In 1813, a number of changes had been made:					
Infantry of the Line					
1st Regiment	Blue	Pink	Red	Blue	White metal
2nd Regiment	Blue	White	Red	Blue	Brass
3rd Regiment	Blue	Yellow	Red	Blue	White metal
4th Regiment	Blue	White	Red	Blue	Brass
Chasseurs	Green	Black	Red	White	Brass

The cavalry was made up of two regiments of Light Dragoons[22] the second dressed the same as the first except

22. See Page 91 for their colours.

1
2
3
4
5
6
7
8
9
10

that their aiguillettes and buttons were yellow and brass respectively; and a troop of Hussars, 48 strong, dressed in the French fashion. These last wore green jackets with red facings, green pelisses trimmed with black lamb's wool and white breeches. The lace and braid was yellow and the buttons were brass.

On 21 May 1807, Murat decided to provide himself with a personal body guard which was called the *Chevau-légers de Berg*. The 1st Squadron was made up of well-to-do volunteers, and was classed as *Garde du Corps*. A further troop was formed and, together with the squadron, went to Spain. After serving as a body guard to Joseph Bonaparte when he went to take possession of his throne, they were incorporated into the *Garde Impériale*[23] in November 1808.

Waldeck–Reuss–Oldenburg –Anhalt

Oldenburg joined the Confederation in 1808 and the other three Principalities in 1807, but none were able to furnish many troops.

Waldeck contributed 400 men in three companies and Reuss 450 men also in three companies, these were combined to form the 2nd Battalion of the 6th Confederation Regiment. The Waldeck troops wore white coatees with dark blue facings.

Oldenburg provided a battalion of 800 men in six companies. The Duchy was incorporated into the Empire in 1810, and this contingent was transferred to the French 129th Regiment of the Line and adopted its dress.

23. See *Lanciers de Berg* above.

CLEVE-BERG

1. Gunner (1812)
2. Chasseur à Cheval (1812)
3. Grenadier (1812)

NASSAU

4. Grenadier (1809) wearing shako which replaced the helmet
5. Fusilier (1810) with shako cover

BADEN

6. Dragoon (1809)
7. Grenadier of the Guard (1806)
8. Officer, Garde du Corps (1813)

1
2
3
4
5
6
7
8

The Principalities of Anhalt-Dessau, Anhalt-Bernburg, and Anhalt-Koethen found 350, 240 and 210 men respectively, and these were joined with the troops from Lippe to form the 5th Confederation Regiment. During the armistice between 3 June and 10 August 1813, a regiment of *Chasseurs à Cheval* was raised. This was only in action at Kulm and was wiped out on 30 August in that year.

Saxony

By the treaty of Posen on 11 December 1806, Napoleon granted the Elector of Saxony the style and title of King. Thenceforth, Frederick Augustus I's fortunes followed those of his powerful protector.

The French defeat in Russia and the retreat that followed brought the Prussian and Russian forces to the frontiers of Saxony. Although often accused by Napoleon of being faint-hearted in carrying out his part of the treaty and despite the fact that his troops deserted at Leipzig in October 1813, Frederick Augustus came under violent attack at the Congress of Vienna. Prussia and Russia both wanted Saxony wiped off the map. In the event, Saxony lost a considerable amount of territory, most of which went to Prussia.

The Saxon Army consisted of Foot Guards, twelve (later eight) infantry regiments, two Light Infantry regiments, a corps of riflemen, a regiment of *Garde du Corps,* two regiments of Cuirassiers, four of *Chevau-légers,* one of Hussars, and units of Foot Artillery, Horse Artillery and Engineers.

CHEVAU-LÉGERS DE BERG (1807–8)

1. Officer
2. Trooper
3. Trumpeter
4. Service dress

3
4
1
2

Infantry of the Line

Until 1810, the infantry wore white coatees with turnbacks of the same colour. The open collar, the lapels and the round cuffs were in the distinguishing colours, as follows:

Regiment	Facing	Buttons
Kurfürst	Scarlet	Brass
Von Sänger	Scarlet	White metal
Prinz Clement	Dark Blue	Brass
Prinz Anton	Dark Blue	White metal
Von Rechten	Purple	Brass
Von Niesemeuschel	Purple	White metal
Prinz Xavier	Light Blue	Brass
Von Ryssel	Light Blue	White metal
Prinz Friedrich August	Grass Green	Brass
Von Low	Grass Green	White metal
Prinz Max	Yellow	Brass
Von Thümmel	Yellow	White metal

After 1810, uniforms of the same cut as those of the German troops on the French side were adopted, namely white coatees with square lapels, closed collars and point cuffs. The white turnbacks and the shoulder-straps were piped with the facing colour. There remained only eight regiments.

The distinctive colours from 1810 and from 1813

Regiments 1810	Facing	Buttons	Regiments 1813	Facing	Buttons
König	Scarlet	Brass	König	Red	Brass
Von Niese meuschel	Scarlet	White metal	Von Niesemeuschel	Red	White metal
Von Low	Blue	Brass	Prinz Anton	Blue	White metal
Prinz Anton	Blue	White metal	Von Low	Blue	Brass
Prinz Friedrich August	Green	Brass	Prinz Maximilien	Yellow	Brass
Prinz Clement	Green	White metal	Von Rechten	Yellow	White metal
Prinz Max	Yellow	Brass	Prinz Friedrich August	Green	Brass
Von Rechten	Yellow	White metal	Steindal	Green	White metal

OLDENBURG

1. Infantry (1815)
2. Officer, Infantry (1810)
3. Private, Infantry (1810)

REUSS

4. Private, Infantry

ANHALT

5. Private, Infantry (1809)
6. Chasseur à Cheval. This regiment was raised on 10 August 1813 and wiped out on 30 August following

6
5
4
1
2
3
L. & F. FUNCKEN

Light Infantry

The Light Infantry was formed from riflemen drawn from the Infantry of the Line. Initially, there were two battalions which were named the 1st and 2nd Light Infantry Regiments in 1810. They wore green coatees with brass buttons, the turnbacks were green and the collar and point cuffs were black, all with red piping. The breeches were grey with red stripes and thigh ornaments.

Chasseurs à Pied

When they were formed in 1810, the *Chasseurs à Pied* were attached to the Light Infantry and wore the same dress except that the turnbacks were of light green, the collar was green with a black patch in front, piped with red, and the breeches were plain grey. The shako plate was in the form of a hunting horn and the festoon was white instead of green.

Grenadiers of the Guard

This regiment retained the traditional colours of the Saxon Guard which was raised in the 17th century. The red coatee with yellow facings was cut in the French style with square lapels after 1810. The long skirts were retained.

Cavalry

SAXONY–INFANTRY I

1. Grenadier N.C.O., Prince Maximilien's Regiment (1810)
2. Drummer, Prince Frederick-Augustus's Regiment (1810)
3. Major, King's Regiment (1810)
4. Light Infantry (1810)
5. Chasseur (1810)
6. Musketeer, Von Low's Regiment (1810)

Regiment	Coatee	Collar and Cuffs	Turnbacks	Buttons
Garde du Corps (1806)	Pale Yellow	Blue	Blue	Yellow (loops)
Cuirassiers of the Guard (1806)	Pale Yellow	Red	Red	
Cuirassiers of the Guard (1810)	White	Red	Red	Brass
Zastrow's Cuirassiers (1806)	Pale Yellow	Yellow	Yellow	
Zastrow's Cuirassiers (1810)	White	Yellow	Yellow	White metal
Chevau-légers or Dragoons:				
Polenz's Regiment	Light Red	Blue	Blue	Brass
Prinz Jean's Regiment	Light Red	Black	Yellow	Brass
Prinz Albert's Regiment	Light Red	Dark Green	Dark Green	Brass
Prinz Clement's Regiment	Light Red	Pale Green	Pale Green	Brass

1
2
3
4
5
6
L. & F. FUNCKEN

In 1810, the same colours were retained, but the coatee had the collar, lapels and point cuffs in the distinguishing colour.

Regiment	Jacket	Collar and Cuffs	Pelisse	Fur Trim	Lace and Buttons
Hussars (1806)	White	Light Blue	Light Blue	Black	White on the pelisse, sky blue on the jacket. White metal
Hussars (1810)	Light Blue	Black	Light Blue	Black	
Uhlans	Coatee	Collar, Cuffs and Turnbacks			Buttons
1811 Prinz Clement's Regiment with lances	Light Red	Light Green			Brass
1813; with blue czapska (lance-cap)	Blue	Black			White metal

Artillery

From 1717, the Saxon Artillery had kept to its traditional colours of green and red. Until 1810, the Foot Artillery wore green coatees with long skirts, and light yellow waistcoats and breeches. After 1810, the uniform was modified and the army was reorganised. Thereafter there was one regiment of Foot Artillery in three brigades, one brigade of Horse Artillery and one battalion of Artillery Train. From 1810, the colour of the breeches became white or grey. The buttons remained brass.

The Horse Artillery wore a coatee of the same colours as the Foot Artillery, but cut like that of the *Chevau-légers*. The cuffs were pointed, the breeches were white and the overalls were grey with red stripes. Instead of leggings, hessian boots with red binding and bosses were worn.

The Artillery Train, which was attached to the Foot Artillery, wore a light blue uniform with black facings and a shako of the infantry pattern. They carried a sword and two pistols.

SAXONY–INFANTRY II

1. Pioneer (1810)
2. Officer, undress (1811)
3. Officer, undress (1812)
4. Grenadier of the Guard (1810)
5. Grenadier, Infantry of the Line, service dress (1811)

1
2
3
4
5
L. & F. FUNCKEN

Cadet Corps

These young soldiers wore long red coats. The collar, which was upright, the lapels, and the cuffs were white and piped with red. The linings and turnbacks and the breeches were white, the buttons of white metal and the leggings were black. The short sword, the musket and bayonet were small and light, proportionate to the size and strength of the cadets who had to use them.

The Saxon Duchies

The five Saxon Duchies (Saxe-Coburg-Saalfeld, Saxe-Gotha-Altenburg, Saxe-Hildburghausen, Saxe-Meiningen, and Saxe-Weimar) joined the Confederation in 1806 and together found 2,800 men who formed the 4th Confederation Regiment, generally called the Regiment of the Saxon Duchies. In 1806, a troop of twenty Hussars took part in the campaign as an escort to the Grand Duke of Weimar's entourage.

The Swiss and the Danish Auxiliaries

The Swiss

Despite the confusion that their red uniforms caused by their resemblance to the British, the Swiss kept to their traditional colour to the end. By the Act of Mediation in 1803, Napoleon reorganised the Helvetian Republic. In the same year, he concluded a treaty which required Switzerland to furnish a contingent of 16,000 men. From these were formed the four Swiss infantry regiments that were raised in 1804 and who were to fight with distinction in the Peninsular and in Russia.

SAXONY–CAVALRY & ARTILLERY

1. Officer, Horse Artillery (1811)
2. Dragoon, Prince Clement's Regiment (1811)
3. N.C.O., Foot Artillery
4. Uhlan (1815)
5. Artillery Trumpeter (1812) with shako cover
6. Hussar (1810)

5
6
4
2
1
3
L. & F. FUNCKEN

Colours, 1804–1806

Regiment	Jacket	Collar, Lapels and Cuffs	Piping	Buttons
1st	Maroon	Yellow	Light Blue	Brass
2nd	Maroon	Royal Blue	Yellow	Brass
3rd	Maroon	Black	White	Brass
4th	Maroon	Sky Blue	Black	Brass

Colours in 1812

The maroon coatee was retained, but turnbacks were white with a maroon grenade for the Grenadiers and a buff hunting horn for the Light Infantry.

Regiment	Collar (piped in maroon)	Lapels	Cuffs	Cuff Slashes
1st	Yellow	Yellow	Yellow	Red
2nd	Dark Blue	Dark Blue piped with red	Dark Blue	Dark Blue piped with red
3rd	Black	Black piped with red	Black	White piped with dark red
4th	Sky Blue	Sky Blue piped with red	Sky Blue	Sky Blue piped with red

The epaulettes were scarlet for Grenadiers; red piped with the facing colour for the Line companies and buff piped with maroon (as was the collar), for Light Infantry. Numerous changes were made in these regulations in the course of the wars.

Danish Auxiliary Corps

The Danish Auxiliaries, commanded by Prince Frederick of Hesse, consisted in 1812 of four regiments of Infantry, two battalions of Rifles, six squadrons of Dragoons, two squadrons of Hussars and four batteries of Artillery.

SAXONY–CAVALRY OF THE GUARD

1. Cuirassier, full dress (1811)
2. Trumpeter, Garde du Corps (1811)
3. Officer, Zastrow's Cuirassiers (1810)
4. Captain, Garde du Corps (1810)

3
4
1
2
L. & F. FUNCKEN

1
2
3
10
9

4
5
6
8
7
L. & F. FUNCKEN

The four Infantry regiments and the Rifles had the following distinguishing colours:

Regiment	Facing Colour
The Queen's	Light Blue
Schleswig (Chasseurs)	Light Blue
Oldenburg	Green
Holstein	Green
Fyeri	White

The Light Infantry wore the same dress as the Infantry of the Line but green with black facings and, from 1810, grey with white brandebourgs.

The cavalry from Holstein, whom we have included with the Dragoons from Jutland, wore a common uniform but with the facings piped with yellow. The Hussars from Jutland wore blue jackets with crimson facings, crimson pelisses with black fur and fawn breeches. The lace and braid was white and the buttons were of white metal. The headdress was a black busby at first, later it was a shako with a red festoon and a white plume.

The Artillery wore a uniform like the infantry with dark blue facings and brass buttons. Their breeches were dark blue.

SAXE-GOTHA (pp. 104–5)

1. Fusilier (1807)
2. Fusilier (1810)
3. Fusilier (1809)

SAXE-WEIMAR

4 & 5. Infantry (1807)

SAXE-COBURG

6. Infantry (1809), the oak-leaves were only worn when specially ordered
7. Fusilier (1809)

SAXE-WEIMAR

8. Carabinier (1812)

SAXE-HILDBURGHAUSEN

9. Infantry (1809)

SAXE-MEININGEN

10. Infantry (1807–12)

DENMARK & SWITZERLAND

1. Grenadier, 3rd Swiss Regiment
2. Grenadier, Prince of Neuchatel's Battalion
3. Voltigeur, Prince of Neuchatel's Battalion
4. Light Infantry, 3rd Swiss Regiment
5. Fusilier, 3rd Swiss Regiment
6. Grenadier, Fyeri Regiment, Denmark
7. Jutland Dragoon (1812–13), Denmark

1
2
3
4
5
6
7
L. & F. FUNCKEN

The Kingdom of Italy

In 1805, the Viceroy Eugène de Beauharnais had the task of organising the forces of the new kingdom and followed the model of the French Army, substituting green for the blue of the French uniforms.

He raised a royal guard consisting of a troop of *Gardes d'Honneur,* a regiment of Grenadiers, a regiment of Rifles, each with a battalion of *Vélites* attached and two regiments of cavalry.

The rest of the army consisted of twenty regiments of Infantry of the Line, ten of Light Infantry and ten of cavalry. Most of these regiments took part in the Russian Campaign.

Italy was divided into five military regions. Two Polish legions, who had gone into the service of the Cisalpine Republic in 1798, rejoined the Grand Army in 1806. These were the last foreign troops to serve in the Italian Army.

ITALY–THE VICEROY'S ARMY

1. Infantry of the Guard
2. Vélite, Chasseurs of the Guard
3. Fusilier, 4th Regiment of the Line
4. Grenadier of the Guard
5. Chasseur of the Guard
6. Grenadier, marching order
7. Dragoon, 2nd Regiment (Napoleon's Dragoons)
8. 2nd Regiment, Chasseurs à Cheval
9. Garde d'Honneur of Bologna

7
8
9
1
2
3
4
5
6
L & F. FUNCKEN

The Kingdom of Naples

Joachim Murat became King of Naples in 1808, and set about organising an army.

Some existing corps formed the basis. There was a regiment of Grenadiers of the Royal Guard and two regiments of *Vélites*. The *Vélites* of a former royal regiment became the Guard Hussars and there was also a mounted *Garde du Corps*.

There were two regiments of Infantry of the Line and these became the 1st King's and the 2nd Queen's Regiments. To these were added a 3rd Royal, a 4th Royal Samite, a 5th Calabrian and so on up to a 9th which had no title, Murat apparently having run out of ideas. Four Light Infantry regiments, some *Chasseurs à Cheval,* and some *Chevau-légers* were raised between 1808 and 1813.

The Artillery was reorganised and brought up to strength. A large force of mounted *Gendarmerie* was raised to put down the increasing menace of banditry. The various shades of red that had been worn in the former army were replaced by purple, a favourite colour of Murat's. A few Neapolitan troops fought in the Peninsula, and also in Germany.

NAPLES–THE ARMY IN 1812

1. Officer, 1st Regiment, Infantry of the Line, undress
2. Bandsman, 3rd Regiment, Infantry of the Line
3. Marine of the Guard
4. Light Infantry, 2nd Regiment, Infantry of the Line
5. Officer, Light Cavalry of the Guard
6. General Officer
7. 1st Chevau-lègers
8. Trumpeter, 1st Chevau-lègers
9. Grenadier, 6th Light Infantry

1
2
3
4
5
6
7
8
9

The Spanish Army

Infantry of the Line, 1805–1811

Regiment	Cuffs and Cuff Slashes	Lapels	Collar	Piping	Buttons
Rey (King's)	Violet	Violet	Violet	Violet	Gold
Reina (Queen's)	Violet	Violet	Violet	Violet	Silver
Principe (Prince's)	Violet	Violet	White	Violet	Gold
Soria	Violet	Violet	White	Violet	Silver
Princesa (Princess')	Violet	White	Violet	Violet	Silver
Savoy	Black	Black	Black	Black	Gold
Crown	Black	Black	Black	Black	Silver
Africa	Black	Black	White	Black	Gold
Zamora	Black	Black	White	Black	Silver
Seville	Black	White	Black	Black	Silver
Cordoba	Red	Red	Red	Red	Gold
Guadalajara	Red	Red	Red	Red	Silver
Majorca	Red	Red	White	Red	Gold
Leon	Red	Red	White	Red	Silver
Aragon	Red	White	Red	Red	Silver
Granada	Sky Blue	Sky Blue	Sky Blue	Sky Blue	Gold
Valencia	Sky Blue	Sky Blue	Sky Blue	Sky Blue	Silver
Toledo	Sky Blue	Sky Blue	White	Sky Blue	Gold
Murcia	Sky Blue	Sky Blue	White	Sky Blue	Silver
Cantabria	Sky Blue	White	Sky Blue	Sky Blue	Silver
Saragossa	Green	Green	Green	Green	Gold
Spain	Green	Green	Green	Green	Silver
Burgos	Green	Green	White	Green	Gold
Asturias	Green	Green	White	Green	Silver
Fijo de Centa	Green	White	Green	Green	Silver
Navarre	Dark Blue	Dark Blue	Dark Blue	Dark Blue	Gold
America	Dark Blue	Dark Blue	Dark Blue	Dark Blue	Silver
Malaga	Dark Blue	Dark Blue	White	Dark Blue	Gold
Jaen	Dark Blue	Dark Blue	White	Dark Blue	Silver
Military Orders	Dark Blue	White	Dark Blue	Dark Blue	Silver
Estremadura	Crimson	Crimson	Crimson	Crimson	Gold
Castilian Volunteers	Crimson	Crimson	Crimson	Crimson	Silver
State Volunteers	Crimson	Crimson	White	Crimson	Gold
Volunteers of the Crown	Crimson	Crimson	White	Crimson	Silver
Bourbon	Crimson	White	Crimson	Crimson	Silver

SPAIN–CAVALRY

1. Hussar, Maria Luisa's Regiment (1808)
2. Spanish Hussars
3. King's Regiment
4. Dragoon, Almanza Regiment (1808)
5. Chasseur à Cheval, Olivera Regiment (1808)
6. Cap badge, Hussars (see 1 & 2)
7. Collar badge, Hussars & Chasseurs à Cheval
8. Collar badge, Cavalry of the Line

7
8
6
1
2
3
4
5
L. & F. FUNCKEN

Light Infantry, 1805–1811

Battalion	Cuffs and Slashes	Lapels	Collar	Piping	Turnbacks	Buttons
1st Aragon	Red	Red	Red	White	Red	Silver
1st Catalonia	Yellow	Yellow	Yellow	Yellow	Yellow	Gold
2nd Catalonia	Yellow	Yellow	Dark Blue	Yellow	Yellow	Gold
Tarragona	Yellow	Dark Blue	Yellow	Yellow	Yellow	Gold
Gerona	Yellow	Yellow	Yellow	Yellow	Yellow	Silver
2nd Aragon	Red	Red	Dark Blue	Dark Blue	Red	Silver
1st Barcelona	Yellow	Dark Blue	Yellow	Yellow	Yellow	Silver
2nd Barcelona	Yellow	Yellow	Dark Blue	Yellow	Yellow	Silver
Barbastro	Red	Dark Blue	Red	Dark Blue	Red	Silver
Valencia Volunteers	Crimson	Crimson	Crimson	Dark Blue	Crimson	Silver
Navarre Volunteers	Crimson	Dark Blue	Crimson	Dark Blue	Crimson	Silver
Campo Mayor	Crimson	Crimson	Dark Blue	Dark Blue	Crimson	Silver

Line and Light Infantry, 1812–1814[24]

Battalion	Collar and Cuffs	Turnbacks and Piping	Buttons	Shako Cords and Plumes	Epaulettes Fringes
Line Grenadiers	Red	Red	Gold	Red	Red
Line Fusiliers	Red	Red	Gold	White	
Line Voltigeurs	Red	Red	Gold	Green	Green
Light Carabiniers	Sky Blue	White	Silver	Red	Red
Light Chasseurs	Sky Blue	White	Silver	White	
Light Voltigeurs	Sky Blue	White	Silver	Green	Green

Dragoons, 1805–1814

Regiment	Collar	Turnbacks	Lapels, Cuffs	Pocket Piping	Collar
King's	Crimson	Red	Crimson	Crimson	White
Queen's	Red	Red	Red	Red	White
Alamansa	Sky Blue	Red	Sky Blue	Sky Blue	White
Pavia	Yellow	Red	Red	Red	Red
Villa Viciosa	Green	Red	Green	Green	White
Sagunto	Yellow	Red	Green	Green	Green
Numancia	Black	Red	Black	Black	White
Lusitania	Yellow	Red	Black	Black	White

24. The dark blue uniform shown in Volume I, page 149, should perhaps have been sky blue although, for more than a century, it has always been depicted as dark blue. The wording of the regulations is obscure and may have led to this confusion.

1
2
3
4
5
6
7
L. & F. FUNCKEN

Cavalry of the Line, 1805–1814

Regiment	Collar	Piping Collar Lapels and Cuffs	Lapels	Cuffs	Lapel Button Holes	Turnbacks	Piping	Buttons
King's	Red	White	Red	Red	Yellow	Red	Red	Gold
Queen's	Sky Blue	Red	Sky Blue	Sky Blue	White	Red	Red	Silver
Prince's	Red	White	Red	Red	White	Red	Red	Silver
Infanta	White	Yellow	White	White	Yellow	Red	White	Gold
Bourbon	Red	White	Red	Red		Red	Red	Silver
Farnesio	Red	Jonquil	Red	Red		Red	Jonquil	Silver
Alcantara	Red	Green	Green	Red		Red	Red	Silver
Spain	Jonquil	Crimson	Crimson	Crimson		Red	Red	Silver
Algarve	Jonquil	Jonquil	Jonquil	Jonquil		Red	Red	Silver
Calatrava	Red	Sky Blue	Sky Blue	Sky Blue		Red	Red	Silver
Santiago	Crimson	Crimson	Crimson	Crimson		Red	Red	Silver
Montesa	Crimson	White	White	Crimson		Red	Red	Silver

The Romana Division

In order to enforce the blockade against the British, Napoleon asked Spain to supply a contingent of troops to protect the German coast. Among the Spanish troops that left their country in 1807 was the division of the Marquis de la Romana, with a strength of 15,000 men.

The usurpation of the Spanish throne by Napoleon's brother and the general train of events in Spain infuriated the Spanish who deserted in large numbers, assisted by the British fleet. On their return, most of these troops were killed at the Battle of Espinosa on 11 November 1808.

Poland

Poles formed the Legion of the Vistula, the Legions of the North and the Krakus, which latter was usually known as the French Cossacks, as well as the Polish Lancers and the Lithuanian Tartars of the *Garde Impériale*.

The Legion of the North

This was composed of Prussian prisoners of Polish origin and, at first, they wore the Prussian uniform. Later, on

SPAIN–INFANTRY (p. 115)

1. Saragossa Regiment, Infantry of the Line (1808)
2. Light Infantry, Cordoba Regiment (1808)
3. Grenadier, Infantry of the Line (1808)
4. Gunner (1808)
5. Gunner (1810)
6. Grenadier, Guadalejara Regiment, Marquis of Romana's Division (1807–8)
7. Grenadier, Princess's Regiment, Marquis of Romana's Division (1807–8)

POLAND

1. Grenadier, 1st Regiment, Vistula Legion (1808)
2. Grenadier, Legion of the North (1806)
3. Lancer, Vistula Legion (1808)
4. Uhlan, 17th Regiment, Grand Duchy of Warsaw (1807–14)
5. Krakus (1813)
6. Hussar, 13th Regiment, Grand Duchy of Warsaw (1807–14)

4
5
6
17
13
1
2
3
L. & F. Funcken

Napoleon's orders, it adopted the Polish-style coat and the *czapka* (lance cap). The Legion was raised in 1806 and it was transferred to the Saxon service as the 5th Regiment of Infantry of the Grand Duchy of Warsaw in 1808.

The Legion of the Vistula

The remains of the Italian Legion were assembled in Westphalia in 1807, and re-formed as the Legion of the Vistula. There were three regiments of Infantry and one of Lancers. These gallant Poles fought in the Peninsular War and in the Russian Campaign, then at Leipzig and finally in France.

The Grand Duchy of Warsaw

The Grand Duchy having erected by the Treaty of Tilsit, an army was organised. There were twenty-two Infantry regiments, three of *Chasseurs à Cheval,* two of Hussars, one of Cuirassiers and fourteen of Lancers.

After the disaster of 1812, Poniatovski[25] tried to reorganise the army and among the new troops, the Krakus from the area of Cracow, appeared. It was the Krakus who gave Napoleon the idea of forming the *Éclaireurs* of the *Garde Impériale.* The Krakus distinguished themselves before Paris, remaining true to the Emperor to the end.

Among the other foreign troops in French service, we should also mention the Irish Legion which became the 3rd Foreign Regiment in 1811; the Regiment of Joseph Napoleon, formed from Spaniards from Holstein,[26] which fought in Italy, Germany and Russia; the Regiment of Catalonia which had a brief existence in 1812; the Regiment of Illyria formed in 1810 from Belgians who had been in the Austrian service; and lastly the Portuguese Legion, made up half of Africans, which was almost wiped out in Russia.

In addition to the Danish Auxiliaries, by the Treaty of Paris in 1812, the French also acquired Prussian and Austrian auxiliaries, 20,000 of the former and 34,000 of the latter. They wore the uniforms of their respective countries.

25. Prince Joseph Poniatovski (1762–1813), Marshal of France, drowned at the passage of the Elster.
26. See above under the Romania Division.

THE SWEDISH, AUSTRIAN AND RUSSIAN ARMIES

Sweden

It was after she joined the Third Coalition in 1805 that Sweden came into conflict with Napoleon for the first time.

After he had come in contact with the French *émigrés* in Germany King Gustav IV of Sweden had come to hate Napoleon. His alliance with the Austrians, Russians and the British cost him his possessions, Pomerania and Stralsund, in Germany. Still worse, Napoleon and Alexander I of Russia, having become reconciled in 1807, wished to force Sweden to break with Britain. When the King of Sweden refused, the Russians invaded Finland and, although repelled several times, eventually forced Sweden to evacuate the country. The unfortunate Gustave IV was deposed and exiled, and was replaced by Charles XIII who signed a peace with Russia in 1809 after his army had been twice defeated.

Charles XIII was courageous and patriotic, but unintelligent and of weak character. Old and without children, he agreed that he should be succeeded by a foreigner, a Marshal of France, who had earned the admiration of the Swedes by the humanity and wisdom which he had shown in his administration of Jutland, Fyen and the Hanseatic Towns which had fallen to the French in 1808.

The Marshal of France was Jean-Baptiste Bernadotte (1763–1844) who enlisted into the *Régiment Royal-Marine* at the age of 17 when he was left the sum of ten louis;[27] was promoted sergeant in 1789, Colonel in 1792, *général de*

27. About 240 francs.

brigade in 1793 and Marshal of France in 1804. As Charles XIV, he ascended the Swedish throne in 1818.

Napoleon's despotic behaviour drove Bernadotte, now the Crown Prince, to ally himself with the Russians in 1812 and with Britain and Prussia in 1813. As Commander-in-Chief of the Army of the North, he had under him the Russian and Prussian forces, as well as the Swedish. Although circumstances forced him to fight against France, Bernadotte took no part in her Occupation, having previously ensured that her natural frontiers would be respected. Despite Napoleon's predictions, Bernadotte not only kept the throne that a strange chance had given him, but he raised a line of democratic Kings who reign to this day.

Austria

The British were anxious to remove the threat of invasion presented by Napoleon's preparations along the Channel coast, and created a diversion by instigating the Third Coalition in 1805. As a result, Russia, Austria, the Two Sicilies and Sweden joined with Britain against France.

Without waiting for the Russians, Austria, bent on avenging the humiliation she had received at the hands of Napoleon in 1797 and 1800, decided upon a surprise attack which was certain of success, according to the Archdukes. A force of 58,000 under General Mack invaded Bavaria while the Archduke Charles with 95,000 men, swept into the plain of the River Po in Italy. A reserve of 22,000 remained in Austria, for use on either front.

The Emperor reacted like lightning. The seven corps of the Grand Army, the cavalry under Murat and the *Garde Impériale* made for the Rhine, while 60,000 men under Prince Eugène de Beauharnais and Massena held the invaders in Italy.

SWEDEN

1. Light Dragoon (1807)
2. Infantry of the Line (1815)
3. Grenadier, Leib-regiment (1807)
4. Artillery Officer (1807)
5. Calmar Regiment, Infantry of the Line (1807)
6. Infantry of the Line (1807)

5
1
6
2
3
4

Surrounded, Mack tried to break out, but found that the French had got between him and the Russians. After being driven back at Wertingen on 8 October, at Memmingen on 12 October and at Elchingen on 14 October, the Austrian general concentrated his forces at Ulm the final battle was to take place.

The Austrians made a sortie on the night of 15–16 October, and Napoleon put in the *Chasseurs à Cheval*, the Mamelukes, and the *Grenadiers à Cheval* of the *Garde Impériale*. They came up against the Latour Dragoons[28] whom the Austrians always used as their advanced guard and whose bravery was legendary.

The victors of Marengo and the Belgian dragoons fought hand to hand and in mud up to the stirrups. So close were they that they struck at each other with the hilts of their swords, for they could not use the points. However their heroism was in vain. Ulm capitulated on 20 October and Mack, in a sodden hat and a muddy greatcoat, marched his defeated army past the Emperor and into captivity. The French took 33,000 men, 18 generals, 40 standards and colours and 60 guns. The Austrians brought Mack to trial and condemned him to death, but the sentence was commuted to two years' imprisonment.

The Archduke Ferdinand, defeated by Murat near Nuremberg, escaped with 2,000 men. On 18 October 1805, he lost 12,000 prisoners, 500 vehicles, four standards, seven generals and the treasure chest.

The Russians reached the Austro-Bavarian frontier only to find the remnants of the army that was to have led them to the Rhine. They headed for Vienna where they awaited

28. Formerly a regiment from the area later to become Belgium, Prince Ferdinand de Ligne's Dragoons.

AUSTRIA–INFANTRY I

1–3. German Infantry (1805)
4. Hungarian Grenadier (1805)
5. Officer, German Infantry (1805)

5
3
1
4
2

the Archduke Charles who was withdrawing his forces from Italy with the utmost speed. Napoleon, however, despite the weather pushed on. Having secured his flanks, he struck routing the Austrian and Russian armies. On 10 November, the French were little more than 60 miles from Vienna and, three days later, their advance guard entered the Austrian capital.

All the same, the Emperor realised that he had not yet gained the day, for the enemy had regrouped their forces after withdrawing over 280 miles in eighteen days and now had 100,000 men in the north, as well as the Russian reinforcements under General Bennigsen?[29] In the south, there were another 100,000 men under the Archduke Charles who posed a severe threat.

Napoleon agreed to an armistice proposed by his opponents and then regrouped his forces, making it appear that he was going to take advantage of the truce and beat a retreat. The Austrians and Russians were taken in and, without waiting for Bennigsen to arrive, fell straight into the trap at Austerlitz on 2 December 1805. Two days later the Austrian Emperor, Francis II, asked for an armistice and, on 26 December, peace was signed on terms even more humiliating than that preceding it.

After what we have just said, one might come to the conclusion that the Austrian Army was hardly fit to be called an army. In fact, up to then it had been one of the finest in the world. It was simply that Napoleon outwitted their undoubtedly inferior leaders. In the years that followed, Napoleon's enemies got the measure of him and eventually defeated him.

29. Augustus de Bennigsen, 1745–1826.

AUSTRIA–INFANTRY II

1. Hungarian Grenadier (1807–15)
2. Hungarian Infantry (1806)
3. German Infantry (1806)
4. German Grenadier (1809–15)
5. Grenadier's cartridge-pouch and sword

1
2
3
4
5

Infantry

In 1809, there were sixty-four infantry regiments, some composed of Austrians of German stock and some of Hungarians. Their uniforms were as follows:

Regiment	Origin	Facing Colour	Buttons
1. Kaiser Franz	German	Bright Pink	Brass
2. Erzherzog Ferdinand	German	Dark Yellow	Brass
3. Erzherzog Carl	German	Sky Blue	White metal
4. Hoch und Deutschmeister	German	Sky Blue	Brass
5. 1st Garrison Regiment	German	Dark Blue	White metal
6. 2nd Garrison Regiment	German	Black	White metal
7. F.M.L. Baron Schröder	German	Dark Blue	White metal
8. Baron Huff	German	Poppy	Brass
9. Graf Clerfayt	Walloon	Apple Green	Brass
10. Baron Kheul	German	Bright Green	White metal
11. Graf Wallis	German	Rose Red	White metal
12. Manfreddini	German	Dark Brown	Brass
13. Reisky	German	Grass Green	Brass
14. Baron Klebek	German	Black	Brass
15. Graf d'Alton	German	Dark Yellow	Brass
16. Baron Terzi	German	Violet	Brass
17. Furst Hohenlohe	German	Light Brown	White metal
18. Graf Stuart	German	Bright Pink	White metal
19. Alvinczy	Hungarian	Sky Blue	White metal
20. Wenzel Kaunitz	German	Lobster Red	White metal
21. Baron Gemmingen	German	Sea Green	Brass
22. Graf Lacy	German	Dark Yellow	Brass
23. Grossherzog von Toscana	German	Poppy	White metal
24. Baron Preiss	German	Dark Blue	White metal
25. Graf Brechainville	German	Sea Green	White metal
26. Baron W. Schröder	German	Bright Green	Brass
27. Graf Strassoldo	German	Dark Yellow	Brass
28. Graf Wartensleben	German	Grass Green	White metal
29. Graf Olivier Wallis	German	Mid-Blue	White metal
30. Prinz of Ligne	Walloon	Light Blue	Brass
31. Benjowsky	German	Dark Yellow	White metal
32. Graf S. Gyulai	Hungarian	Sky Blue	Brass
33. Graf Sztaray	Hungarian	Dark Blue	White metal
34. Furst A. Esterhàzy	Hungarian	Poppy	White metal
35. Baron Wenkheim	German	Lobster Red	Brass
36. Fürst U. Kinsky	German	Light Grey	White metal
37. Baron de Vins	Hungarian	Poppy	Brass
38. Herzog Ferd. von Württemberg	Hungarian	Rose Red	Brass
39. Thomas Nadasdy	Hungarian	Poppy	White metal

AUSTRIA–CAVALRY I

1. Hussar (1806)
2. Light Dragoon (1812)
3. Cuirassier (1806)
4. Uhlan (1805)

1
2
3
4
L. & F. FUNCKEN

Regiment	Origin	Facing Colour	Buttons
40. Graf Mittrowsky	German	Crimson	White metal
41. Baron Bender	German	Lemon	White metal
42. Graf Erbach	German	Orange	White metal
43. Graf Thurn	German	Lemon	Brass
44. Graf Belgiojoso	Italian	Dark Yellow	White metal
45. Baron Latterman	German	Crimson	Brass
46. Baron Neugebauer	German	Dark Blue	Brass
47. Graf F. Kinsky	German	Grey-Green	White metal
48. Baron Schmidfeld	Hungarian	Grey-Green	Brass
49. Graf Pellegrini	German	Light Grey	White metal
50. Graf Stain	German	Violet	White metal
51. Baron Splenyi	German	Dark Blue	Brass
52. Erzherzhog Anton Victor	Hungarian	Bright Pink	Brass
53. Johann Jellacié	Croatian	Bright Pink	White metal
54. Graf Gallenberg	Croatian	Apple Green	White metal
55. Graf Murray	Walloon	Mid-Blue	Brass
56. Graf W. Colloredo	German	Grey-Green	Brass
57. Graf J. Colloredo	German	Light Grey	Brass
58. Baron Beaulieu	Walloon	Black	White metal
59. Jordis	German	Orange	Brass
60. Ignaz Gyulayi	Hungarian	Grey-Green	White metal
61. Saint Julien	Hungarian	Grass Green	Brass
62. Franz Jellacié	Hungarian	Grass Green	White metal
63. Erzherzog Josef Franz	Walloon	Dark Green	White metal
64. Chasteler (Chasseurs)	German	Grey Uniform	

There were also seventeen regiments of Frontier Guards and a corps of *Chasseurs*. In addition, there were various bodies of volunteers and *francs-tireurs*. The famous Andreas Höfer was the leader of the Tyrolese uprising in 1809. He was born in 1767 and, after being betrayed, was shot on Napoleon's orders in 1810.

Cavalry

The cavalry was composed of *Cuirassiers*, Hussars, *Uhlans*, Dragoons, and *Chevau-légers*. After 1805, the last two classes wore white or green coats. The uniforms of the others are given below:

AUSTRIA–CAVALRY II

1. Uhlan (1815)
2. Private, Landwehr (1809)
3. Officer, Cuirassiers (1815)
4. Chasseur (1809)
5. Hussar (1813–15)

5
3
1
2
4
L. & F. FUNCKEN

● Cuirassiers

Regiment	Collar and Breeches	Collar and Cuff Slashes and Piping	Buttons
Kaiser Franz	White	Dark Red	White metal
Erzherhog Franz Josef	White	Black	White metal
Herzog Albrecht	White	Bright Red	Brass
Kronprinz Ferdinand	White	Grass Green	White metal
Sommariva	White	Light Blue	White metal
Liechtenstein	White	Black	Brass
Lothringen	White	Dark Blue	White metal
Hohenzollern-Hechingen	White	Scarlet	Brass

● Hussars (yellow and black and lace braid);

Regiment	Pelisse and Jacket	Breeches	Shako	Buttons
1. Kaiser Franz	Dark Blue	Dark Blue	Black	Brass
2. Erzherzog Josef Anton	Light Blue	Light Blue	Dark Yellow	Brass
3. Erzherzog Ferdinand Carl	Dark Blue	Dark Blue	Ash Grey	Brass
4. Hessen-Homburg	Bright Green	Bright Red	Bright Blue	White metal
5. Radetzky	Dark Green	Carmine	Dark Yellow	White metal
6. Blankenstein	Cornflower	Cornflower	Black	Brass
7. Liechtenstein	Light Blue	Light Blue	Grass	White metal
8. Kurfürst von Hessen	Bright Green	Bright Red	Black	Brass
9. Frimont	Dark Green	Carmine	Black	Brass
10. Stipsicz	Light Blue	Light Blue	Grass	Brass
11. Szeckler	Dark Blue	Dark Blue	Black	White metal
12. Palatinate	Cornflower	Cornflower	Black	White metal

● Uhlans

Regiment	Czapska	Jacket	Facing Colour	Buttons
1. Merveldt	Dark Yellow	Grass Green	Scarlet	Brass
2. Schwarzenberg	Grass Green	Grass Green	Scarlet	Brass
3. Erzherzog Carl	Scarlet	Dark Green	Scarlet	Brass

AUSTRIA–WEAPONS & HEADDRESSES

1. Infantry helmet as worn up to 1805
2. Shako (1806)
3. Shako (1811)
4. Shako (1815)
5. Hussar shakos
6. Cavalry helmet from 1805
7 & 8. Grenadier caps
9. Hussar's carbine
10. Cavalry pistol
11. Infantry musket
12. Chasseur's carbine with long bayonet
13. Hussar's sword
14. Cuirassier's sword

9
10
1
2
3
4
5
6
7
8
11
12
13
14

A 4th Regiment of *Uhlans* was raised in 1813, and wore white *czapkas*. Finally, we come to the Artillery, who wore fawn uniforms cut in the infantry style. The guns were painted with yellow ochre.

Russia

The army that Catherine II formed[30] had gradually changed since her death. Under Paul I, it lost its typically Russian character though the traditional green of the uniforms, which dated from the time of Peter the Great, remained.

When Alexander I came to the throne in 1801, he discontinued the practice whereby General Officers were allowed to call their regiments by their own names, and the regiments resumed the territorial names that they had previously used.

RUSSIA–INFANTRY OF THE LINE I

1. Grenadier with full equipment (1805–7)
2 & 3. Grenadier, marching order (1807–8)
4. Grenadier, winter uniform (1808–10)

The dark green of the Russian army's uniforms was almost black; the same colour was used for those Cavalry regiments who had green uniforms

Infantry

The Russian infantry was completely reorganised in 1805 into thirteen regiments of Grenadiers, eighty-three of Musketeers and twenty-six of *Chasseurs*.

● Infantry of the Line (1805)

Regiment	Collar and Cuffs	Shoulder-Straps	Pompom Centre
	GRENADIER REGIMENTS		
The Tzar's Regiment	Red	Red	Red
Pavlov	Red	White	White
Petersburg	Turquoise	Red	Red
Tauride	Turquoise	White	White
Iakaterinoslav	Light Green	Red	Red
Little Russia	Pink	Red	White
Kiev	Pink	White	
Kherson	Lilac; later Dark Green	Red	Red

30. See *Arms and Uniforms II–18th Century to the Present Day*.

1 2 3 4

Regiment	Collar and Cuffs	Shoulder-Straps	Pompom Centre
Siberia	Lilac; later Dark Green	White	White
Caucasia	Mid-Blue	Red	Red
Moscow	White	Red	Red
Phanagoria	White	White	White
Astrakhan	Orange	Red	Red
	MUSKETEER REGIMENTS		
Veliko-Loutsk	Yellow	Red	Red
Neva	Yellow	White	Yellow
Riazan	Yellow	Yellow	White
Ielets	Red	Yellow	Turquoise
Kexholm	Red	Raspberry	Yellow
Bieloserk	Red	Turquoise	Light Green
Tenguin	Red	Rose	Rose
Lithuania	Red	Light Green	Light Green
Sievsk	Turquoise	Yellow	Turquoise
Sofia	Turquoise	Raspberry	Grey
Revel	Turquoise	Turquoise	Light Green
Tobolsk	Turquoise	Rose	Light Green
Dnieper	Turquoise	Light Green	Rose
Tchernigov	Turquoise	Grey	Yellow
Toula	Light Green	White	Light Green
Pskov	Light Green	Yellow	White
Mouromsk	Light Green	Raspberry	Light Green
Rostov	Light Green	Turquoise	Yellow
Nisov	Light Green	Pink	Pink
Arkhangelsk	Light Green	Light Green	Turquoise
Old Inkermanland	Light Yellow	Red	Yellow
Riask	Light Yellow	White	Turquoise
Viborg	Light Yellow	Yellow	White
Apcheron	Light Yellow	Raspberry	Light Green
Azov	Light Yellow	Turquoise	Red
Smolensk	Pink	Yellow	Yellow
Briansk	Pink	Raspberry	Light Green
Ladoga	Dark Green	Yellow	Pink
Vladimir	Dark Green	White	Light Green
New Inkermanland	Dark Green	Pink	Lilac
Alexopol	Dark Green	Raspberry	Light Green
Koslov	Dark Green	Turquoise	Grey
Iaroslav	Dark Green	Yellow	Turquoise
Nijegorod	Dark Green	Red	Yellow
Bielevsk	Pale Coffee	Red	Yellow
Sebastopol	Pale Coffee	White	Light Green

RUSSIA–INFANTRY OF THE LINE II

1 & 2. Grenadier (1809–11)
3. Musketeer (1805)
4. Grenadier in greatcoat (1812–15)
5. Grenadier, summer uniform
6. Musketeer, winter uniform (1812–15)

3
4
1
2
5
6

Regiment	Collar and Cuffs	Shoulder Straps	Pompom Centre
Troitsk	Pale Coffee	Yellow	Red
Vitebsk	Pale Coffee	Raspberry	White
Sousdal	Mid-Blue	White	Yellow
Tiflis	Mid-Blue	Yellow	Light Green
Kabardinski	Mid-Blue	Raspberry	Turquoise
Kazan	Mid-Blue	Turquoise	White
Polotsk	White	Yellow	Light Green
Perm	White	Raspberry	Yellow
Ouglitch	White	Turquoise	Turquoise
Koursk	White	Pink	Pink
Voronej	White	Light Green	Light Green
Moscow	Raspberry	Red	Red
Boutirsk	Raspberry	White	Turquoise
Kolivan	Raspberry	Yellow	Pink
Novgorod	Raspberry	Raspberry	White
Viazma	Raspberry	Turquoise	Yellow
Narva	Raspberry	Pink	Light Green
Poltava	Raspberry	Light Green	Light Green
Navajinski	Orange	White	Light Green
Tambov	Orange	Yellow	Light Green
Ukraine	Orange	Raspberry	Grey
Schlusselbourg	Orange	Turquoise	White
Nachelbourg	Orange	Pink	Yellow
Orlov	Orange	Light Green	Turquoise
Saratov	Orange	Grey	Lilac
Staroskol	Orange	Lilac	Pink
Olonets	Orange	Dark Blue	Dark Blue
Riga	Camel	Red	Red
Oufa	Camel	White	White
Iakaterinburg	Camel	Yellow	Yellow
Chirvanski	Grey	Red	Red
Tomsk	Grey	White	White
Seleguinski	Grey	Yellow	Yellow

Regiment	Collar and Cuffs	Shoulder-Straps
REGIMENTS FORMED IN 1803		
Pernov	Red	Grey
Koporsk	Turquoise	Turquoise
Volhynie	Light Green	Grey
Podolsk	Light Yellow	Pink
Galits	Pink	Turquoise
Crimea	Dark Green	Dark Blue
Vologda	Dark Blue	Light Green

RUSSIA–INFANTRY OF THE LINE III

1. Chasseur (1805–7)
2. Chasseur (1808–9)
3. Chasseur (1811)
4. Officer, Chasseurs (1809–11)
5. Private, Marines (1811)
6. Drummer, Grenadiers (1805–7)
7. Drummer, Grenadiers (1811)
8. Subaltern, Grenadiers (1812–15)
9. Subaltern, Grenadiers, service dress (1814–15)

1
2
3
4
5
6
7
8
9

REGIMENTS FORMED IN 1806:	Collar and Cuffs	Shoulder-Straps
Kalouga	Turquoise	Lilac
Mohilev	Light Green	Grey
Kostroma	Light Green	Lilac
Vilna	Light Yellow	Light Green
Estonia	Pink	Turquoise
Odessa	Dark Green	Grey
Pensa	Light Yellow	Grey

The following ten regiments of Musketeers, which were raised in 1806, had five buttons, instead of three, on the cuff-slashes:

Regiment	Collar	Cuffs	Cuff Slashes	Shoulder-Straps
Libau	Light Blue	Red	Red	Red
Kamchatka	Red	Red	Red	Red
Mingrelie	Yellow	Yellow	Red	Red
Vilmanstrand	Red	Red	Red	White
Brest	White	Red	Red	Yellow
Kremenchoug	Yellow	Red	Red	Yellow
Minsk	Light Blue	Red	Red	White
Neuchlot	Yellow	Red	Red	White
Okhotsk	Light Blue	Light Blue	Red	Yellow
Petrovsk	White	Red	White	Light Blue

In 1807, all collars and cuffs became red. The infantry was formed into divisions, and the appropriate number appeared on the shoulder-strap. The Grenadiers' mitre-caps were given up, except in the Pavlov Regiment, they retained them until 1914.

● Chasseurs

The *Chasseurs* wore a light green uniform with collar and cuffs in the facing colour:

Regiment	Collar and Cuffs	Piping
1	Light Yellow	
2	Pink	
3	Red	
4	Grey	
5	Turquoise	
6	Brown	
7	White	
8	Mid-Blue	

RUSSIA–CUIRASSIERS

1. Non-Commissioned Officer (1803–7)
2. Subaltern (1812–17)
3. Trooper, full dress (1812–17)
4. Service dress (1809–11)
5. Helmet with ear-muffs (1803–7)
6. Helmet (1809)
7. Cartridge-pouch, Their Majesties' Regiment
8. Cartridge-pouch, other ranks

5
7
8
6
3
1
2
4
L. & F. FUNCKEN

Regiment	Collar and Cuffs	Piping
9	Yellow	
10	Black	
11	Apricot	
12	Light Raspberry	
13	Pale Coffee	
14	Chestnut	
15	Iron Grey	
16	Camel	
17	Violet	
18	Maroon	
19	Lilac	
20	Dark Green	
21	Red	White
22	White	Red
23	Orange	White
24	Light Green	Light Blue
25	Light Yellow	Red
26	Dark Blue	Red

Cavalry

In 1806, there were six regiments of *Cuirassiers,* thirty regiments of Dragoons, eight regiments of Hussars, one regiment of Tartar horse and one of Polish horse. The *Chasseurs à Cheval* were raised in 1812.

● Cuirassiers

The Cuirassiers wore white coatees with the collar, cuffs and turnbacks in the facing colour. The helmet, which had replaced the hat, was made of black leather with a thick black hair crest on the comb. Ear-muffs were worn in winter. The forage cap was of the infantry pattern with the band in the facing colour.

● Colours in 1805:

Regiment	Facing Colour	Buttons
His Majesty the Emperor's	Light Blue	White metal
Her Majesty the Empress's	Light Raspberry	White metal
Military Orders	Black	Brass
Little Russia	Green	Brass
Gloukov	Mid-Blue	White metal
Iekaterinoslav	Orange	White metal

RUSSIA–DRAGOONS

1 & 2. Dragoons, dismounted duties
3. Dismounted duties from 1808
4. Private (1814)
5. Working dress (1814)

4
5
1
2
3
L. & F. FUNCKEN

It was not until 1807 that queues were discontinued in the Cuirassiers. The former thick crest on the helmet was replaced by one of short, stiff black hair, except for the trumpeters who had red. In review order, the officers retained the old style of helmet. In 1812, a 'browned' steel cuirass was introduced. At the same time, the Pskoff and the Starodoub Dragoons were converted into Cuirassiers, the former having raspberry facings and brass buttons, and the latter having light blue facings.

●Dragoons

The thirty regiments of Dragoons constituted the cavalry of the Line in the Russian Army and, in 1806, six new regiments were raised.

The Dragoons had the following distinctions:

RUSSIA–HUSSARS

1. Trumpeter (1814–15)
2. Full dress (1813)
3. Winter dress with cloak (1806)
4. Full dress (1803–6), the red leather patches on elbows were to prevent wear
5. Trumpeter, White Russian Hussars (1809–11)
6. N.C.O., Irkoutsk Hussars (1813–17)
7. Sword and sabretache, other ranks (1812)
8. Shako, original model
9. Carbine (1809)
10. Low shako with 'distinction' badge (1812)

Regiment	Facing Colour	Buttons
Riga	Red	Brass
Starodoub	Red	White metal
Kharkov	Orange	Brass
Sieversk	Orange	White metal
Tver	Bright Blue	Brass
Tchernigov	Bright Blue	White metal
Saint Petersbourg	Rose	Brass
Moscow	Rose	White metal
Smolensk	Yellow	Brass
Kinbourn	Yellow	White metal
Pskov	Brown	Brass
Kargopol	Brown	White metal
Vladimir	Pale Coffee	Brass
Nijegorod	Pale Coffee	White metal
Taganrog	Grey	Brass
Marva	Grey	White metal
Orenburg	Black	Brass
Inkermanland	Black	White metal
Irkhoutsk	White	Brass
Siberia	White	White metal
Kazan	Light Raspberry	Brass
Kiev	Light Raspberry	White metal
Courlande	Turquoise	Brass
New Russia	Turquoise	White metal
Borisoglievsk	Violet	Brass
Pereiaslav	Violet	White metal
Livonia	Red piped with white	Brass
Jitomir	Red piped with white	White metal
Finland	White piped with red	Brass
Mitau	White piped with red	White metal

1
2
3
4
5
6
7
8
9
10

REGIMENTS FORMED IN 1806	Facings	Buttons
Tiraspol	Red	Brass
Iamburg	Red	White metal
Niejine	Turquoise	Brass
Arsamas	Turquoise	White metal
Serpoukhov	Yellow	Brass
Dorpat	Yellow	White metal

● Hussars

The Hussars were dressed in the Hungarian style with patches of red leather at the elbows and round the button-holes to save the material from wear. On the march, grey or buff overalls were worn over the white breeches. In 1805, they wore the following distinctions:

Regiment	Pelisse	Jacket	Collar and Cuffs	Braid	Buttons	Sabretache and Badges
Soum	Turquoise	Yellow	Turquoise	White	White metal	Turquoise and White
Pavlograd	Turquoise	Dark Green	Turquoise	Yellow	Brass	Dark Green and Yellow
Elisavetgrad	Light Yellow	Light Yellow	Red	Yellow	Brass	Red and Yellow
Mariopol	Dark Blue	White	Yellow	Yellow	Brass	White and Yellow
Alexandria	Black	Black	Red	White	White metal	Black and White
Olviopol	Dark Green	Dark Green	Dark Green	White	White metal	Dark Green and White
Isioum	Dark Blue	Red	Dark Blue	White	Brass	Dark Blue and Yellow
Akhtyrsk	Maroon	Maroon	Yellow	Yellow	Brass	Maroon and Yellow
White Russia	Dark Blue	Dark Blue	Red	Red and White	White metal	Dark Blue and White
Grodno (1806)	Dark Blue	Dark Blue	Light Blue	Red and White	White metal	Dark and Light Blue
Loubny (1807)	Dark Blue	Dark Blue	Yellow	Red and White	White metal	Dark Blue and White

RUSSIA–CHASSEURS À CHEVAL & UHLANS

1 & 2. Chasseurs à Cheval (1813–14)
3 & 4. Uhlans (1809–15)

1
2
3
4

In 1809, the hussars had the following distinctions:

Regiment	Pelisse	Jacket	Collar and Cuffs	Braid	Buttons	Breeches	Sabretache and Badges
Soum	Grey	Grey	Red	White	White metal	Red	Red and White
Pavlograd	Turquoise	Dark Green	Turquoise	Yellow	Brass	Dark Green	Dark Green and Red
Elisavetgrad	Grey	Grey	Grey	Yellow	Brass	Dark Green	Dark Green and Red
Mariopol	Dark Blue	Dark Blue	Yellow	Yellow	Brass	Dark Blue	Dark Blue and Yellow
Alexandria	Black	Black	Red	White	White metal	Black	Black and Red
Olviopol	Dark Green	Dark Green	Red	White	White metal	Red	Dark Green and Red
Isioum	Dark Blue	Dark Green	Red	White	White metal	Dark Blue	Dark Blue and White
Akhtyrsk	Maroon	Maroon	Yellow	Yellow	Brass	Dark Blue	Maroon and Yellow
White-Russia	Red	Dark Blue	Red	White	White metal	Dark Blue	Red and White
Grodno	Dark Blue	Dark Blue	Light Blue	White	White metal	Dark Blue	Dark and Light Blue
Loubny	Dark Blue	Dark Blue	Yellow	White	White metal	Dark Blue	Blue and White

●Uhlans

The regiments of horse were, in fact, Lancers and wore the traditional Polish dress which was copied by many other countries. The jacket was of dark blue with lapels, cuffs and turnbacks of crimson, a favourite colour of the Poles.

The first regiment to be converted into *Uhlans* was the Grand Duke Constantine's[31] in 1803. A fourth regiment, that of Volhynia, was raised in 1807, when the four were given the title of Uhlans.

●Colours in 1805:

Regiment	Collar	Collar Piping	Czapska	Czapska Braid
Lithuanian	Dark Blue	Crimson	White	Crimson
Tartar	Dark Blue	Crimson	Crimson	White
Polish	Crimson	Dark Blue	Dark Blue	White

RUSSIA–IMPERIAL GUARD

1. Cuirassier (1813–14)
2. Chevalier Garde (1804–6)
3. N.C.O., Horse Guards (1804–5)
4. Hussar (1802–9)
5. Uhlan (1809–11)
6. Chasseur à Cheval (1814–16)
7. Dragoon (1809–12)

SHABRAQUES

8. Cuirassiers
9. Chevalier Garde
10. Horse Guards
11. Hussars
12. Uhlans
13. Chasseurs
14. Dragoons

31. The younger brother of Tzar Alexander I, he fought in Italy and at Austerlitz.

1
2
3
8
9
4
5
10
11
13
12
14
6
7

The Volhynia *Uhlans* had scarlet facings with a dark blue *czapska* braided with mixed yellow and scarlet. In 1806, the Tchougouiev Cossacks were converted into *Uhlans* and were given collars and facings of red and red *czapskas* with white braid.

In 1812, seven Dragoon regiments followed suit. Their distinctive colours were:

Regiment	Collar and Facings	Epaulettes	Buttons	Czapska	Czapska Braid
Iamburg	Crimson	Yellow	Brass	Crimson	Yellow
Orenburg	Crimson	Yellow	Brass	Crimson	Yellow
Jitomar	Red	White	White metal	Blue	White
Siberia	Red	White	White metal	White	Red
Vladimir	Blue Collar Red Facings	Yellow	Brass	Blue	Yellow
Taganrog	Blue Collar Red Facings	Yellow	Brass	White	Red
Serpoukhov	Blue Collar Red Facings	Yellow	Brass	Red	Yellow

●Chasseurs à Cheval

Chasseurs à Cheval were reintroduced in 1812 when Alexander I converted eight regiments of Dragoons. The uniform was the same as before, apart from the pointed cuffs in the facing colour.

Regiment	Facing Colour
Livonia	Red
Pereiaslav	Crimson
Sieversk	Orange
Dorpat	Rose
Tiraspol	Yellow
Tchernigov	Ultramarine
Arsamas	Mid-Blue
Niejine	Light Blue

The Imperial Guard

The Imperial Guard dated from the time of Peter the Great who surrounded himself with a band of like-minded friends and eventually formed them into a military body. In 1700 there were two regiments, by 1730 there were four and,

RUSSIA–ARTILLERY & COSSACKS

1. Fusilier, Foot Guards (1812–15)
2. Gunner, Foot Artillery (1809)
3. Gunner, Horse Artillery (1814)
4. Gunner, Foot Artillery of the Line (1809)
5. Gunner, Horse Artillery of the Line (1814)
6. Cossack of the Guard in winter caftan
7. Don Cossack with demi-caftan (1815)
8. Ural Cossack (1812)
9. Kalmuk (1812)

1
2
3
4
5
6
7
8
9

under Paul I, there were ten corps composed of Infantry, Cavalry and Artillery. The Napoleonic Wars led to the formation of additional corps to which soldier were transferred as a reward for bravery.

● Foot Guards

The Foot Guards wore the same dress as the Infantry of the Line but with distinctive loops round the button-holes of yellow lace with lines of the distinguishing colour of the regiment. Their uniform developed along parallel lines. In 1811, the Foot Guards adopted the same organisation as the Line with flank companies (Grenadiers and Light Infantry) and centre companies (Fusiliers who were the equivalent of the Musketeers of the Line). The *Chasseurs* of the Guard had a company of *Carabiniers* (Sharp-shooters). In 1811, the Foot Guards consisted of three ordinary regiments and three of *Chasseurs*.

In 1813, the Czar's Grenadiers and the Pavlov Grenadiers were transferred to the Foot Guards. At this time, too, a Supply Column and an Engineer battalion were added to the Imperial Guard.

● Household Cavalry

In 1805, there were two regiments of Cuirassiers, one of Hussars and one of Cossacks. In 1813, a regiment of *Uhlans* and one of Dragoons was added and finally, in 1814, a regiment of *Chasseurs à Cheval*. All these regiments wore a dress similar to that of their counterparts in the line, but with badges peculiar to the Guard.

Artillery

In 1805, there were eleven regiments of Artillery organised in twenty-four brigades, of which three formed the reserve. By 1815, the number had increased to twenty-eight regiments and thirty-three independent companies. Their uniform was like that of the infantry, but with black facings. The Horse

Artillery wore a uniform similar to that of the Dragoons, likewise with black facings.

The Artillery of the Imperial Guard wore the same dress as that of the line, but with the distinctive badges of the Guard. It consisted of a battalion of Foot Artillery and a troop of Horse Artillery known collectively in 1811, as the Guards Artillery Brigade. The Horse Artillery wore the heavy cavalry helmet with the 'Guards Star' as a badge until 1812, when they adopted the shako with a uniform of the *Chasseurs* pattern. The gun-carriages and ammunition-waggons were painted light green.

Cossack Irregulars

The Guard Cossacks were styled Regulars, whilst those of the line were called Irregulars. The Cossacks came from seven regions: the Don, the Black Sea, Siberia, Orenburg, the Urals, Astrakhan, and the Bug. In return for exemption from taxation, these soldiers were required to serve up to an advanced age unless sickness or infirmity rendered them unfit.

Their uniforms were as follows:

Regiment	Jacket	Collar and Cuffs	Headdress	Plume	Sash	Trousers	Lance Pennon
Don (The Hetman's)	Dark Blue Caftan[32] Half-caftan	Piped Sky Blue	Black fur cap, Red bag	White, Black and Orange	Edged Light Blue	Dark Blue and Light Blue Stripes	*None*
Black Sea	No regulation uniform, short jackets with loose sleeves and Red tassels; pistols, musket and lance without pennon						
Astrakhan	No regulation uniform, usually dressed Kirglish style; bow and arrows						
Orenburg	Dark Blue Caftan	Raspberry	Black fur cap, Crimson bag	White, Black and Orange	Edged White	Dark Blue with Raspberry stripes	Raspberry and White
Urals	Raspberry Caftan	Laced White	Tall Crimson cap, fur edges	*None*	Black Leather	Sky Blue with White stripes	*None*
Siberia	Dark Blue Caftan	Red	Black fur cap, Red bag	White Black and Orange	Edged Sky Blue	Dark Blue with Red stripes	White and Regimental colour

32. The *caftan* was a form of pelisse; the half-caftan was worn in summer.

Regiment	Jacket	Collar and Cuffs	Headdress	Plume	Sash	Trousers	Lance Pennon
Tchougouiev (Uhlans after 1808)	Dark Green caftan or kurta with Red collar, Dark Green cuffs, White braid and Cossack cap						
Boug	Dark Blue Kurta	White, cuffs piped in White	Black fur, White and Blue cords	White and Black tip	White	Dark Blue with White stripes	
Ukraine (1st Regiment)	Dark Blue Caftan	Crimson	Cossack cap, White cords in 1815	White in 1815	Dark Blue with Raspberry stripes	Grey with Raspberry stripes	Crimson and White
Kalmuks	Dark Blue Caftan	Red	Yellow Polish cap with Black fur trim		Light Blue	Blue with Red stripes	

The Bashirs were of Mongol stock like the Kalmuks, they had no regulation uniform and carried whatever weapons they preferred. These Cossacks were undoubtedly the strangest troops to fight in the Napoleonic wars, they struck fear into the hearts of all who beheld them during their wild charges.

APPENDIX

The Belgians at Waterloo

The Allies were received with joy by the Belgians as many of them had fallen in battle in the Imperial armies, but the liberators behaved just as badly in Belgium as they did in France. The popular reaction, thought to be a demonstration of pro-French feeling, led some of the leading Belgians to propose to Austria that Belgium should be re-united with the Austrian Empire on a semi-autonomous basis like that

THE BELGIANS AT WATERLOO

1. Private, centre company
2. Private, flank company
3. Officer, 8th Hussars
4. 2nd Carabiniers
5. 5th Light Dragoons

4
5
3
1
2
L. & F. FUNCKEN

which had existed before the French Revolution. They were very shaken to learn that Napoleon had already decided upon Belgium's future: she was to be amalgamated with the United Provinces of the Netherlands (that is, Holland).

The Dutch Government took over the Belgian Legion that had been raised by the Austrians. The regiments retained their identity and, in the case of the cavalry, their dress, while the infantry that fought at Waterloo wore a transitional uniform, although, in the ordinary course of events, they would have adopted the Dutch uniform. The Belgian infantry battalions, composed mostly of recruits who had never been in action, acquitted themselves honourably in the final battle although they were called upon to play only a small part. The 7th Battalion of the Line distinguished itself particularly, and was presented with banners by the townships of Tournai and Oudenarde. On 21 April 1815, the Belgian *Carabiniers, Chevau-légers* and Hussars had been converted into the 2nd *Carabiniers,* the 5th Light Dragoons and the 8th Hussars. They did not play a very distinguished role in the Battle of Waterloo as they fled the field fairly early on, despite the efforts of their officers.

INDEX